D1608762

*When They Ask for Bread*

# when they ask for bread

*or*
*pastoral care*
*and counseling*
*in everyday places*

by
GEORGE BENNETT

JOHN KNOX PRESS
ATLANTA

Library of Congress Cataloging in Publication Data

Bennett, George, 1931–
  When they ask for bread.

  Bibliography: p.
  Includes index.
  1. Pastoral psychology.  2. Pastoral theology.
I.  Title.
BV4012.B39      253      77–15743
ISBN 0–8042–1159–0

To Clarence Y. Barton and David A. Steere

## Acknowledgments

I appreciate the influence, support, and encouragement I have received for the writing of this book from my parents, family, colleagues, students, friends, parishioners, and editors. I thank Mary Jane who suggested the title. I especially appreciate the helpful work of Dr. Clinton D. Morrison and the typing done by Martha Lee Johnson.

# Foreword: How to Read This Book

This book is written for busy pastors. But it also contains information and techniques useful to those in other helping professions—teachers, nurses, social workers, volunteers, etc. Almost anyone may benefit from this book personally.

The book is mostly in short segments. These segments are designed to be read in a few minutes each day. Lengthy periods of reading would probably tire the thoughtful reader. Some sections offer suggestions that need to be practiced before the next section is undertaken.

Reading Parts III and IV might turn out to be more valuable if the reader puts some of the suggestions from Parts I and II into practice first. If you have already tried most of these, you will have no trouble in moving on to the later parts of the book. If, however, you find this to be a new approach, I would suggest that it would be worthwhile to explore some of the possibilities before moving on into the more difficult sections. Trying out your wings as you go will probably help you to get more out of the book.

The age-old idea that theory is completed by practice is applicable here. In pastoral care, this is sometimes called a "clinical" approach. This theory simply recognizes that you can understand the theory a lot better if you practice at each stage of your progress.

In this sense, the reader may find that the later sections of this book are more complex. They are for those who have tried their hand with the first ideas and who are ready for more.

Mastering the seemingly simple early parts of the book may increase your power of awareness of what is actually transpiring between people. Then, as you complete the later sections, you will feel better about your work and yourself because you will be continuing to improve your practice of our great helping profession.

# Contents

## Introduction: When They Ask for Bread

"Or what man of you, if his son asks him for bread, will give him a stone? Or if he asks for a fish, will give him a serpent?"

Matthew 7:9–10

All of our training, piety, dedication, and learning may lead us to do exactly the opposite of what we are called to do. We may discover that when people ask for bread, spiritual, psychological, or otherwise—we may unintentionally give them stones.

The purpose of this book is to provide, from the disciplines, theories, and practices of pastoral theology, guidance toward giving people "bread" rather than "stones," when they ask for bread.

The early sections of the book indicate the necessity for ascertaining what people want of pastoral or other helping consultants. The fact is underscored that if we offer something people do not want, their needs are not met and in Milton's language, "The hungry sheep look up, and are not fed." Their response is one of polite ingratitude. Our reaction to such ingratitude is despondency. We begin to question not only our professional but also our personal worth. Knowing what is being asked of us is imperative for competent consulting and confident consultants.

A list of eight kinds of things people seek is outlined and illustrated. As the consultant talks with people, she or he should remain alert to determine and clarify precisely which level the consultee seeks. Otherwise, confusion and discouragement will result.

9

*part I*
# The Importance of Knowing What People Want

## 1. Why Ministers Get Despondent

There are innumerable reasons why ministers get despondent. Some of these have their roots in the remote recesses of their unconscious minds, in the "games" they play, in any of a hundred other factors. But one major reason ministers with whom I talk get despondent is that they feel they have been well prepared and highly trained to provide a service no one wants.

The average seminary graduate has a mastery of exegetical, historical, doctrinal, and philosophical theology, plus hermeneutical homiletic skills. He or she is also trained in church administration, Christian education, and the basic types of pastoral counseling. An M.Div. or a D.Min. degree represents all this training. What does she or he get most of the time in what Charles Merrill Smith called the "first miserable parish"?

"Reverent, I hope you're praying for me—my bunions are sooo painful these days, especially when I have to stand in line at the checkout counter." Or,

"Isn't it awful about Tom Brigand's girl. She had all her hair cut off and kinked—just like a nigger's."

Ministers get despondent because they are not equipped to put their good training to work when and where they are called upon to do so. Attention to the ideas and suggestions in this book will curb if not eliminate this factor in the lives of ministers who wish to be successful (in the best sense of the word) in the great profession of ministry.

## 2. "We had hoped He was the One . . ."

I am going to let you in on a secret. All who meet you—from the most severely diseased to the most confidently successful person—consciously or unconsciously hope that YOU are *the* one. Not "the One to redeem Israel" —but the one to solve their problems and enable them to enjoy fullness of life.

They may be unaware of this hidden hope. They may ignore you, flatter you insincerely, treat you with contempt. They may keep their distance, embarrass you with overfamiliarity, joke foolishly, be suspicious of you, or try to use you. They may relate to you in any of a dozen other ways. Inside, whether they know it or not, they harbor the hidden hope that you may help them.

How you respond to people will determine whether or not you will be of help, temporal, eternal, or both.

I am tempted to say the art of helping people can never be learned from a book. But that is a cop out. Anything can be learned from a book if one wants to learn—how to fire a gun, swim, build a thermonuclear device, nurse an infant, or cook. Practice is essential, but the essentials can be outlined in a book. If you really want to learn how to consult in supermarket aisles and barnyards, this book tells you. The practice to (near) perfection is up to you.

The important fact is that people do want you to help. They really do hope that *you* are *the* ONE.

## 3. *The* **Sine Qua Non** *of Consultation: Style*

The style in which one provides help when help is requested is of greatest import. A few experts feel that one's style and manner is more important than one's "school" of therapy, or to put it colloquially, "Freud cured people, not because he discovered the oedipus complex, but because he knew how to relate to people."

Blunt, accusing, arrogant, authoritarian approaches to people are almost never of value. There may seem to be exceptions to this rule, but these will be clarified in appropriate sections later in this book.

Politeness, socially conventional manners, initial formality are always effective in maintaining a semblance of open communication. The conventions and rituals of good manners may convey initial "stuffiness." But they also communicate respect for persons. The use of formal address, Mr., Mrs., Ms., Miss, may evoke an immediate "please call me by my first name," but seldom evokes defensiveness or resentment.

Open-ended questions are essential in all circumstances except perhaps during intensive cross-examination of a "hostile witness" in a court of law. Closed-ended questions, such as "You really want to suffer, don't you?" generate anxiety and defensive anger, closing the possibility for thoughtful consideration.

Open-ended questions allow people room to "back off," to reflect, to marshal the emotional strength to accept upsetting ideas, "threatening" possibilities. "You know, there is one theory that might, or might not, apply. Sometimes people have hidden, or unconscious, inclinations to make atonement. Does that idea make sense, not that you need to agree that it might apply to you?"

Another almost always successful style is that of discovering parallels in one's own life experience to the behavior or problems of one's consultees. "I hope this comparison does not offend you, but I think you and I are alike in several ways. For one, I have a tendency to bring suffering on myself. Eating too much, for example. I know I'm miserable every time I overeat. Yet, time and again, I'll do it. It's maybe a hang-up with me, I think. Stuffing myself with rich food, then having indigestion. It's almost as if I *wanted* to pay for enjoying myself. I'm wondering if you maybe do the same thing with getting overly committed to too many projects, or promises to people, then suffering with the consequences?" Incredibly, almost all consultees are flattered by such odious comparisons, and tend readily to accept the possibility of truth in such insights.

That without which there is no helping, the *sine qua non* of helping, is a gracious style.

## 4. Finding Out What People Want

This is the most crucial segment of this book. Despair arises when communication between people fails. When an infant cries the mother (or father) *must* know what the infant wants and needs, if anger, grief, or guilt are not to ensue. Trial and error plus hard-won experience is the way a father learns what an infant wants. Although it may seem that a mother knows intuitively what an infant wants, this is not so. The mother also learns by trial and error. She, in our chauvinistic society, ordinarily just has more opportunity to learn by trial and error.

With pastoral consultation the trial-and-error method is not necessary (except with non-articulate infants). Pastors can *ask* what a person wants of them.

In my supervision of pastors in their counseling, I am amazed at the number of times pastors ask me, the supervisor, what a client is asking for. My standard response is, "You have the right question, but you're asking the wrong person." Fifty-nine percent of the time people know what they want and will tell you if you ask them.

So, the first principle in consultation is:

Find out what people are asking.

There are diplomatic ways of ascertaining this.

"I'm sorry to learn about your bunions, but I'm wondering if you are asking anything of me besides prayer?"

"That is startling news about Tom Brigand's daughter's hair. Did you have anything in mind I might do?"

Brutal, "confrontative" questions, like "So what?" or "What do you expect me to do about that?" are counterproductive—except in certain circumstances which will be discussed later.

The important thing is to FIND OUT WHAT PEOPLE ARE ASKING OF US.

Sometimes what people really want is not what they may seem to want. As indicated earlier, the consultant who misses the vital *actuality* of what a person wants can end up feeling a frustrated failure, despondent over her or

14

his inability to succeed at the practice of consultation. The following example illustrates this point.

"Hi, Rev. Doing a little hardware shopping, I see."

"Yes. How are you doing?"

"Well, now that you ask, I'm pretty, well, frustrated, you might say?"

"Frustrated?"

"Yeah. You know I'm going on twenty-nine and I just cannot understand why I never meet a girl, a woman, I could get interested in."

"You can't meet the 'right' girl, huh?"

"Exactly. I know it must sound dumb to you, but really . . . I mean Mother and I were wondering the same thing the other evening. We've talked about it before."

"How is your mother?"

"Oh, you know, she's OK. She gets pretty lonely with me at work all day. She looks forward to the weekends when I'm there to keep her company. I feel like I owe her a lot and I'm just glad to be a comfort to her. It must get pretty lonely all right, all day with no one to talk to, that sort of thing. She sure appreciates it when you come by."

"She seems to miss coming to church services. I've suggested several times that we could arrange for someone to pick her up during the week to come to the circle meetings. They get together pretty often down there—rolling bandages, sorting the Mission Closet clothing, and so on. She never seems to feel up to attending."

"Naw. She kind of likes to stay at home. But home gets lonely during the week."

"Does she have much time to talk on the telephone with some of her friends?"

"None of them ever call anymore. She feels like she shouldn't call them —'if they wanted to talk to me, they'd call,' is the way she feels about it."

"Yeah, I guess I can appreciate that. But—well, I tried to call a few weeks back and the 'intercept' I think they call it in the phone company, came on with a recorded message that the number was no longer in use. I wondered about that."

"Oh, that. Well, she was getting calls from peddlers, people asking for contributions, and so on. She had me get the number changed and unlisted. Keeps her from being annoyed so much."

"I didn't know about that. We'll have to get the number for our office directory."

"Well, no, I mean, she really doesn't want to give the number out. I mean why go unlisted unless you are going to stick with the plan, huh? [laughs] I call her a couple of times each day. On my coffee breaks at the office. At least she gets to hear from *someone* that way. Anyway, she was wondering too, the other night, why I can't ever seem to meet the right girl. I sure get frustrated."

"I thought you and the Glenns girl were friends. I remember when you were in the choir she used to drop you off after practice."

"You mean Greena? Yeah. Mom didn't care for her, you know. See, Mother is, well, kind of old-fashioned. Greena is divorced and Mother doesn't, well, approve of divorcées."

"Oh. Well, where have you been going to meet some, shall we say, 'eligible' young women?"

"Those awful singles places are strictly out. I understand that all those women are interested in is sex and your money. I wouldn't want that kind of person *at all!*"

"I mean, like, well, like down at Central Church, you know that's a pretty big congregation—not like ours—and they must have, oh, dozens of people in their UYP fellowship."

"What's UYP?"

"It means Unattached Young People—they pronounce it 'Yup.' "

"Probably full of pious virgins or something. I wouldn't be interested in any women like that!"

"Well, I thought—anyway, there are several girls, young women in our own choir who—"

"I never really cared for the musical type anyway—too emotional, if you know what I mean."

"I see."

"I guess I'll never know why I can never meet a decent, right sort of girl!"

"There is a commercial service thing. You know—they advertise on television, during the late movie. You call in and they send you an application and you fill it out and their computer matches you with—"

"I never watch television—except the educational station once in a while. Besides, I think computerization is one of the major evils of our times, don't you?"

"I have to admit I get a little peeved when my credit card companies get me 'lost' in the computer."

"Well, I have to get this plunger home. It's been great of you to try to help me. But I'll have to admit that you haven't helped me a bit in solving my problem. Why oh why can't I ever meet a girl?"

"The cashier is kind of cute here in the store, don't you think?"

"Oh, I suppose if one were interested in someone with a lowly position such as a *cashier* in a hardware store, maybe. Hurmph!"

"I understand her dad owns the store and she's working her way through the university here on Saturdays. She's National Honor Society you know."

"I abhor intellectual snobs myself."

"She's a cheerleader too, her father said."

16

"Fat lot he'd know about such things. Besides, athletics get entirely too much emphasis. It's the mind that counts. No sluts for me!"

"Bless you, son."

The young man in the above consultation obviously did not want suggested solutions to a "problem." He wanted to report a "complaint," or "concern."

The consultant missed this and no doubt ended up feeling frustrated, foolish, perhaps a failure, because the consultant did not ascertain what the young man was asking.

Ascertaining what people really want is at least half, if not most of the battle in effective consultation. Sometimes people are unaware of what they want. When the consultant assists them in making this determination, both feel real help has taken place. The following conversation took place in the waiting room of a physician's office.

"It may be none of my business, but are you sick, Reverend?"

"No. Not really. Just getting an overdue checkup."

"I don't really think I'm sick either. But I don't know what else to do. The doctor says he thinks I'm just a little nervous and depressed. He says it's nothing to worry about."

"You do seem a little worried, however."

"I know. Everything physical seems OK. Everything else seems all right. Great really. We've caught up with our debts. We actually have money in the bank. The kids are about launched, as they say. I have this part-time job. We don't need the money. The house is better than it has ever been. That's because the kids and even Edgar have gotten to the point where they take care of their things—keep their rooms neat and so on. And, of course, we have a maid now. She does the cooking on nights we eat in. We eat out a lot. But something doesn't feel right about me. I'm bored actually. I've done, am doing volunteer work and we turn down party invitations we have so many. I don't even enjoy the Club anymore. I'm just—well, I just don't know what I want."

"You feel something is lacking, but you don't know what?"

"That's right. Exactly. If I could just figure out what I want I wouldn't feel so . . . so . . ."

"Empty?"

"Yeah. Empty, kind of. Like I've done everything, have everything. Only there's something missing."

"There is a theory that people who live almost exclusively by 'oughts' with very few 'wants' have a gradually increasing sense of unfulfillment."

"That—well, that's probably not the case with me. You know, well, I have *not* always done what I ought. I had this thing about a year ago. There was this mechanic at the garage where I take the cars when they need oil and things. We got to be friends. We, you know, talked a lot. We met for drinks and things. For a while I really felt alive and . . . well fulfilled. But that wasn't it either. It wasn't Everlasting Love after all. Sort of a Spring Affair, you might say. After a time we both knew it. Knew that wasn't it."

"In other words, having money, things, success, the house and all—the children turning out well—none of that is what is lacking? Not even—er—new love interest, sex and that sort of thing?"

"No. Edgar and I are OK. That's what's so dumb about all this. I have —we have, everything. Only I'm not satisfied."

"One thing thou lackest?"

"I guess I want ME to amount to something. *Me!* [pause] I guess that really sounds selfish, doesn't it?"

" 'Selfish?' Did you know that I have a small garden? Not much really— no time for anything big. Just enough for a few things during the summer. Well I planted some corn. The stalks are tall, rich, and green. There's been a lot of sun and enough rain. We weed and spray. The corn has Everything! But by golly, that corn seems hell, excuse me, heaven-bent on having *ears.* Can you imagine that? It has Everything, yet it is still insisting on producing ears of corn for us to eat!

"Does that sound selfish of the corn?"

"[Laughing] You make it sound so simple. I have everything too. Only I want to—to *produce*—on my own. That really isn't selfish. That's what I'm all about I guess. I want *me* to produce! Not babies, or a clean house, or volunteer work. Edgar has made all that possible. I want ME to produce, Myself!

"I don't know what yet. I used to want to be a nurse. I've thought about going back to school. So many things. But they all seemed pointless. If something were to happen to Edgar, the insurance and all would take care of us. But that's not the point, is it? The point is ME. Producing! That's what I want.

"You know, I don't feel like seeing the doctor today after all. I need to go think about this. I may want to talk with you some more sometime.

"Nurse! Oh, nurse! I want to cancel my appointment now. I've got some thinking to do. And I need to talk with my husband.

"Thank you, Reverend. I hope your checkup is fine."

Nurse to pastor: "She sure seems happy all at once. You may go in now. The doctor is ready to see you . . . "

Assisting people to discover what they want may be half the battle—or all the battle.


## 5. Some People Need Recognition

Scientists have determined that people need recognition. Infants, deprived of recognition, usually in the form of physical touch, become severely ill and may die if they are not recognized by being held, caressed, cuddled. Older persons usually receive recognition by verbal means, by being looked at, talked with.

Some of us have a greater need than others for recognition. Since my days in grade school, through high school, I have sought, and usually received, more than average recognition. I have been elected president of classes and fraternities, and ordained a minister. I relish, even need periodically, to attend a party or meeting, to walk through a cafeteria, and have a number of people greet me, notice me, speak to me. Others who may feel more secure seem less in need of so much "stroking."

But all of us need recognition. Often when we are approached by parishioners or others, they ask no more than some polite form of recognition.

"Reverent, I hope you're praying for me—my bunions are sooo painful these days, especially when I have to stand in line at the checkout counter."

"I'm sorry to learn about your bunions—but I'm wondering if you are asking anything of me besides prayer?"

"Oh, no. It's just nice to feel that you are thinking of me."

"I assure you that I do think about you."

The above exchange can avoid the minister's attempt to offer more than the parishioner asks. Such clarification can prevent confusion to the parishioner and frustration to the pastor. Without clarifying what the parishioner is asking, the minister might try to offer something not wanted at the time. This would cause problems in communication at least, more serious problems possibly. ("That new minister is an odd one. I mentioned that I had bunions and he tried to psychoanalyze me right there in the supermarket aisle. He must have some kind of hang-up.")

One of the popular "put-downs" of our time is the expression "He just wants attention." What is wrong wanting (or needing) attention? Nothing!!

One of our doctoral students conducted a lavish research to find out what people wanted from their pastors. Personal interviews, control-groups, complicated charts, transactional diagrams, in over two hundred pages of typescript yielded the plain fact that most of the time what people want is recognition, to be taken seriously. They do not seek the resolution to eternal riddles, the Answer to unanswerable questions, the panacea for pandemics. They want to be noticed, appreciated, taken seriously as persons.

What a relief to busy pastors! Atlas can shrug or not—the pastor is not expected to bear all the cares of all the people in and out of this world!

The basis of the Christian faith is God's recognition of people. Christ is "Emmanuel, God with us." The ultimate appreciation of our need for recognition is God's becoming (in his inscrutable wisdom, before the foundation of the world, etc.) one of us. With us.

When people seek recognition, they seek what God knows we must have.

19

Ministers, Christians, are to be as "little Christs" to one another, to use Luther's language. When we move among the people, recognizing people, in response to their need for recognition, we are proclaiming the good news, not just in word, but in deed.

An extremely important part of our work, God's work, is recognizing people in the places to which we are called, among those to whom we are sent. This is a significant aspect of pastoral consultation.

## 6. Sometimes They're After Information

Many people approach you with a desire for information. Not just recognition or attention. Not analysis. Not solutions to problems, but information.

The request for information takes many forms. Often the request is simple, direct, uncomplicated.

"Who is a good doctor for bunions?"

"Do you know anybody who has found something that helps their bunions?"

"Where could Tom find out why his daughter acts that way?"

At other times, the request for information is less direct.

"I wish I knew someone who got their bunions cured."

"I suppose there are a lot of books that tell about raising teenagers."

At times the seeker of information speaks paradoxically.

"I believe there is no way to cure the kind of tiredness I experience."

"Teenagers are crazy."

The important work, if you are to be helpful, is to "check out" or confirm the possibility that a person really is seeking information. This is done by simple question or statement.

"Would you like me to recommend a doctor, or are you asking something else?"

"I think you are wondering how Tom might get some information, or how you might get some information, as to why his daughter has done this."

If the person confirms this request for information quickly, readily, then information is probably what they seek. If they respond with hesitation, by changing the subject, or in other nonconfirming ways, they may seek something other than information.

## 7. Advice

Many of us have been brought up on adages such as "advice is cheap" or sarcastic Socratic philosophies such as "Did *you* ever follow anyone's advice?"

Sophisticated and analytic theories, as well as getting "burned" a few times, make most of us wary of offering advice.

There are times, however, when people really want to be advised. Again, the important step is to clarify what people are asking. A safe rule of thumb is not to *offer* advice, but to *provide* advice when we are convinced advice is requested.

There are three circumstances under which providing advice is appropriate. If the answer to any of the following questions is in the affirmative, and if you are convinced that advice is what the person really seeks, then give advice.

Are you qualified by training and accreditation to give the advice? For example, if the question has to do with legalities, only members of the state bar are qualified to advise. If the question is medical, the possession of an M.D. degree is required. Bankers are qualified to give financial advice, etc.

Are you qualified by successful personal experience to give the necessary advice? Should the question be legal and you know certain attorneys of good repute, then your advice should be in the nature of a referral to them. If the question has to do with leading a Sunday school class and you have done that successfully, then your personal experience is a sound basis for advising.

Are you sufficiently *un*involved emotionally in the area of concern to give objective advice? For example, if you have recently had a regrettable and unsatisfactory experience with your automobile, you may not be sufficiently objective to give reasonable advice as to whether someone should purchase a new automobile, or have their used car repaired. Or, if a relative or in-law seeks advice, emotional involvement may inhibit best advice.

## 8. Catharsis

Next to recognition and attention, more people need an opportunity to ventilate crammed up feelings than any other consultation service. I have known professionals and trained semi-professionals who have made a very comfortable income by providing no service other than the opportunity for people to unload frustrations and feelings. Their clients almost universally appreciated such a service. I call this practice "going into Dumping, Inc." There are serious ethical questions with such a practice, and some dangers which will be outlined below.

The fact remains, however, that many, many people want no more than the chance to unload feelings. Often this is all they really need. The pastoral consultant should be prepared to provide such opportunity.

For example, the wife whose mother-in-law visits two weeks each year, whose mother-in-law irritates her to a considerable degree, is probably better off "blowing her stack" to an objective consultant than at the dinner table "in front of the children." If the mother-in-law moves in for keeps, that may be a different matter, but the opportunity for catharsis is often desperately needed. This may be an imperative first step toward more significant help.

The dangers of providing only opportunity for catharsis are threefold. At times people need to change their behavior, life-style, or "script." The strength to do so can be dissipated by allowing them to drain their feelings regularly, thus warding off the "buildup" necessary for more important actions. A man married to a severely neurotic woman whose behavior harms him, their children, and others may be "helped" to put off getting her to needed therapy by letting him talk out his frustrations regularly. This can deprive a number of people, including children, of a chance for a healthier, more satisfactory, more fulfilling life. This can also keep the wife in chronic suffering and pain.

Another danger inherent in "Dumping, Inc." is that seriously disturbed people may be hurt—assisted toward irrevocable and tragic decisions and actions. This will be detailed in the section on Despair and should be carefully noted.

The other danger is at least equally sinister. There are people who cannot tolerate emotional closeness. The opportunity to release emotions freely may make such persons feel terrifyingly vulnerable, that they have been overexposed. They may panic and become physically dangerous to themselves or violent with others. Specific aids in avoiding such harmful, even fatal, results are detailed in the section on Suspicion later in this book.

## 9. The Desire for Feedback

There are times when people want to know what you think of them. These times are rare. It is important, as emphasized earlier, to be certain that people really do want to hear what you have to say about them. If you are only half-convinced, clarify. Telling people what you think of them is risky business. You can make an enemy for life unless you know what the other person wants and how you can go about providing it.

"I" messages are usually more accurate and maintain communication more effectively than "you" messages. For example,

"I find myself getting irritated when you take so long to relate an incident. I notice myself doing this quite often. I'm not sure you are aware of this effect on me." As opposed to,

"You obviously take delight in antagonizing people. You must be awfully insecure to have to go around constantly making everybody angry by dragging out your stories so. Why do you always want to get people upset or mad?"

The former "I" message invites reflection, consideration of possibilities.

Responses take form as follows: "I do not intend to irritate you, I just want to be sure you understand the details exactly. My family have said the same kind of thing to me, only not so diplomatically. Maybe I *do* like to be sure people listen to me, and getting a strong response does reassure me. I've never really thought about that before. Do people sometimes like to make other people angry?"

The "you" messages put the other person on the defense, causing them to feel attacked, and evokes resentment, especially if the messages have some validity. "You're just like my family. They are always getting mad at me and accusing me of being insecure. Well, you can all go to blazes!"

Since few of us are infallible, we are ethically bound to offer any feedback as tentative, open-ended. We seldom have a 100% accurate impression of anyone, including ourselves. Part II of this book is an outline of various personality modes of relating. This will provide a framework for evaluating people. We should not use these concepts or technical terminology to "label" people. Labels are important in the keeping of official hospital records, and serve as shorthand for communication among trained professionals. But labels degrade and dehumanize people when used directly, whether the labels are theological ("sinner!"), psychoanalytic ("latent homosexual"), psychiatric ("schizophrenic"), sociological (O.W. ["out-of-wedlock"]). People can't do anything with labels, other than fear them, resent them, or ask what the hell you mean.

People *can* use feeling-feedback, dynamic explanations. To illustrate this, consider which of the following, if directed toward you, would lead to a desire for further understanding and conversation:

"You're a sinner!" or, "I think you have done something which society and religion do not accept, and you may or may not feel guilty. In any event, we could talk about how to overcome the consequences."

"Obviously, you're a latent homosexual" or, "I feel you to be a sensitive person, with a very human longing for friendship that may be upsetting to you, even frightening, at times. I sometimes know a lot of people who are bewildered by inner sensitivities. Talking may be useful."

"You may be inclined toward a schizophrenic reaction" or, "I recognize you as a person who seems to lack strong feelings at times, who may think deeply at times, and finds that others do not always understand your thoughts. I feel you to be the way I am when I experience great loneliness or fear, or get lost in my thoughts."

"You're O.W." or, "I believe the circumstances of your birth and early life have caused you to wonder if you are as good as other people. I suppose we all have a tendency to blame ourselves for regrettable circumstances over which we had no control. How do you feel about these impressions?"

There are times when the careful employment of labels can be quite helpful.

But for the most part, the giving of feedback when requested should be a diplomatic and "truth-spoken-in-love" procedure in any consultation.

A final warning about the giving of feedback when requested. People who ask what we think of them do not automatically promise to do anything about what we tell them. If all they want is our appraisal, and we assume they intend to make changes in themselves on the basis of our evaluations, we may be setting ourselves up for disappointment. To expect others to do something about themselves or their life-style because we've granted their request for feedback is similar to expecting someone who has asked us the temperature to then do something about the weather.

The following example of a "barnyard" consultation may provoke questions within you regarding your own attitude and moral conviction. Nevertheless, the important point for this section is that this is one example of a combination "information and feedback" consultation. The legal, psychiatric, and moral issues involved are considered in other sections of this book.

"Hello, up there."

"Hi, Pastor. Wait until I throw down the last of this bale of hay and I'll be right with you."

"Just stopped by to see how you folks are getting on. Your mom said you were in the barn."

"Yes. Uh, is something wrong? I mean did you want to talk to me about something?"

"Just ask how you're getting along."

"Oh, uh, just fine. I mean just fine. I mean what could be wrong? I'm just fine. I mean you haven't come to talk to me about anything, have you?"

"Well, no. But you seem to think there is something I ought to be talking to you about . . ."

"Oh, no. Everything is just . . ."

"Is there something you'd like to talk to me about?"

"Oh, no. No. Nothing. I mean nobody's said anything to you have they? I mean about me or anything?"

"Oh, your mom said you seemed worried lately, but I guess moms notice those sorts of things. Is there something?"

"Oh, no. I mean what could be worrying me? I, uh, well of course what with the work here and going to school and all. And, well, you know, there's things that, well, you know, worry a guy."

"Things that worry a guy?"

"Well, if you've got a minute, there is this one thing. Not to do with me, you understand. But I have been worried. About something that's well, that's been a worry. It's nothing, really, I guess. I mean I did sort of mention it to, well to someone down at the school. I don't know if, well . . . I'm not sure if I should talk to a pastor about this."

"Go ahead, if you like."

"Well, I just wondered what, you know, what religion says about . . . about, well it's kind of about . . . sex."

"Religions, most of the 'good' religions, say sex is normal, 'God created . . . and saw that it was good,' that sort of thing."

"No, I don't mean men and women. I mean, well, you know, there's other kinds of sex."

"Are you asking what I think of people who are involved in or tempted to be involved in homosexual activity?"

"Well, yes. Not that it has anything to do with me, but you know, guys wonder about such things."

"I have personal opinions. A lot of brilliant people over the years have advanced different theories. Some think homosexuality is a crime. Others believe it to be a sickness. I personally feel it is a normal stage in human development. My experience is that in one degree or another, boys of a certain age seem attracted to the idea of comparing how far they can urinate, whose is bigger, that sort of thing. That naturally leads to experimentation of a sexual nature. A number of people now believe that homosexuality is a way of life that is natural for many people.

"In any event, everyone has a right to decide what is right as God leads him or her. The Bible says believing in Jesus Christ as Lord and Savior is what makes us 'OK,' whatever our sexual orientation may be.

"For example, if some of your friends, or you, for that matter, were to engage in homosexual experimentation, I would not condemn them or you. A lot of people do not agree with my belief—but what I would say to a homosexual or to you is quite simple, 'Don't be ashamed, and don't do anything to harm yourself or others in any violent way.'

"Wow! I didn't mean to preach a whole sermon. What was it you were asking me?"

"Just what you told me. I'm thirsty. Mom has a pitcher of iced tea and plenty of lemon and sugar. Let's go get some, Pastor."

"Fine. When you want some more feedback, let me know."

"Sure. I don't think Mom's going to be so worried about me being worried so much from now on."

## 10. Behavior Change

Most of us are nagged by chronic problems, some major, some minor. We would like to meet someone who would let us know how we might resolve those problems, without too much personal effort on our part, of course. We may wait a long time, be "taken in" by quacks, pray without result, and sooner

25

or later realize that no one else is going to remove our difficulties—that *we* are going to need to make change in ourselves.

When we reach such a point we are ready for what the transactional analysts call a "change contract." Some experts feel this is the dividing line between seeking "care" and seeking "cure" (therapy).

When a person has reached such a point, made a decision for "cure" instead of other kinds of consultation, you must be ready to provide yourself for their use in attaining the desired change.

We have learned from the transactional analysts and behaviorists in psychological technique that almost all desires for changed behavior fall into one of two categories.

One such category is that of wanting to "get rid" of something—being "frigid," being financially troubled, having endless arguments, drinking, eating, gambling to excess, etc. The second category is that of wanting to succeed at something—be more emotionally responsive, make more money, budget more wisely, control weight, remain sober, etc.

The thoughtful consultant will evaluate the request for assistance in change. The desired change must be reduced to as simple and direct a form as possible. Does the client want to quit eating or drinking entirely, or just cut down? What is meant exactly by "frigid" or "financially troubled"? Does the person wish to *stop* arguing, or *win* arguments quickly?

When the person can state in a simple, short, direct sentence exactly what is to be gotten rid of, or what success really means, specifically, a second major step must be worked out.

This is the process of arriving at readily observable behavior that will indicate whether or not the counselee is attaining the desired change. Often an imperative "piece of behavior" is to consult an expert in the area of change desired. Such experts probably cannot be contacted in the supermarket aisle or barnyard. But the *program* for doing this can be decided anywhere. For example, the person who wishes to change his or her sexual responsiveness should agree first of all to make an appointment with a medical doctor to rule out the possibility of a medical cause of the problem. Until that behavior is carried out, talking about other aspects of the person's difficulty may be fruitless.

The individual with financial troubles should see a banker or other financial consultant, such as those employed by reputable loan companies. People who start diets should do so under medical supervision since some diets are quite harmful to people with some disorders. If legalities are involved, an attorney's opinion is essential. Educators are important "change agent" specialists, etc.

One benefit of some kind of referral for consultation by an expert is the protection given the pastoral consultant. Shared responsibility is "safer" for the pastor. More so for the consultee!

26

A second value in such an initial behavioral procedure is that it gets the person moving in the direction of desired change gradually. Talking with a doctor or banker is not as difficult as dieting, stopping drinking, cutting up credit cards, or keeping one's mouth shut. Success in an easier "first step" gives people confidence for more difficult steps in making behavioral change.

An easy initial homework assignment or two can have amazing results. For example, I once talked with a busy neurologist who wanted to stop chewing his fingernails. He had had enough psychiatry and enough analytic theory to realize the unconscious dynamic was no doubt repressed rage turned against the self. What he wanted to do was stop biting his nails.

His first behavioral "change" was the purchase of a nail file.

His second was to carry a card in his shirt or laboratory coat pocket at all times. On the card was written, "don't bite them this time." Each time he felt the urge to chew his nails, or caught himself doing so, he was to take out the card, read it, put it back, fondle the nail file in its leatherette case. He "lost" two nail files and sent three cards through the hospital laundry, but eventually he enjoyed using the file "so my hands didn't resemble claws."

Simple, "easy" first steps that led to a meaningful success.

Further behavioral changes should be agreed upon. These should be evaluated frequently and discussion of dynamics involved will naturally emerge. The consultee will be thinking about her or his change practices, especially failures. Often the failures give rise to the most rewarding conversations. Later sections in Part IV will amplify this stage of consultation.

The crucial factor in establishing observable behavior change is the participation of the consultee. If the consultant decides a person should stop using credit cards and requires the agreement of the consultee, the stage is set for failure. That part of the consultee which doesn't agree (the rebellious Child, in transactional terms) will undermine the effort. The *consultee* should do the work of suggesting behavior to be observed. This stage of consulting may consume much time for reasons detailed in Part III.

"Do you mind if I sit here on the swing with you for a visit?"

"No. Nothing seems to matter much these days."

"Sounds like you're having a bad day."

"Bad life is more like it."

"Tell me about it?"

"Pain. I'm in pain all the time. I have been for a long, long time. Not physical pain. Feelings pain. Know what I mean?"

"I think so. Give me an example, then I'll know for sure."

"Oh, I don't know. It's not anything exactly. I mean I'm confused about it. I'd just like to get rid of feeling so bad so much of the time."

"Give me a specific example."

27

"Well, it sounds kind of dumb. I feel foolish talking to you about it, wasting your time."

"I appreciate your sensitivity. Give me an example, unless it's none of my business."

"Oh, I don't mind telling you about it. I've got to do something. I can't stand it much longer."

"Uh-huh. And the example?"

"It's my husband. You know he drinks too much. We've talked about it, and he's sorry when he gets drunk, and he says he'll quit and for a while he does. Then it happens again. And again. He's lost two jobs. I don't make enough at the store to pay all the bills and he gets down, so he drinks some more. Today they came to turn off the electricity. Last month they took the telephone out. There's not enough now for the kids' school lunches. For food really. I'm so sick of worrying and hurting!"

"You want to quit hurting, emotionally?"

"Sometimes I worry so much I think I'll lose, am losing, my mind! Do people ever go crazy over worrying?"

"If the worries are based in reality, and the pain, I would not think an expert would consider you 'crazy' for wanting to get rid of the worry and the pain."

"How can I get rid of the pain?"

"The answer is easy for me to tell you. You'll probably need some help in carrying out the solution."

"Tell me!"

"Give up that which causes you the most pain."

"But I *love* him!"

"That's why I think you'll need some help."

"You mean if I want to get rid of my pain, I'll have to give up loving him? Give *him* up?"

"That seems the obvious change *you* can make. He might be willing to make some changes . . ."

"We've been through that. Alcoholics Anonymous. A psychiatrist. We even talked with a lawyer about divorce—I thought that might change his mind. He doesn't want to change. He has all the fun and I do all the worrying. When he gets to the point of worry, he takes it out in anger on me and the kids. And he drinks some more. And gets fired. He'll never change."

"He may. We're talking about you right now. Maybe you'll want to think this over some."

"Yes. I'd have to think about it. I guess I *would* need help. In giving up that which causes me the most pain. Can we talk some more about this? I feel better already."

As this consultation progresses, referral to a banker for financial advice,

28

discussions of how to learn to live "alone," when to change what behavior, etc., will require time and effort. There will be failures. But change from being in pain to feeling good can ensue step by step.

## 11. Personality Reorganization

Extensive training and certification by a nationally reputable psychiatric or psychoanalytic society, the Association for Clinical Pastoral Education, the International Transactional Analysis Association, the American Association of Pastoral Counselors, etc., is prerequisite for this level of consultation. The dangers of "messing with" personality are legion and obvious, and the consequences of attempts by inadequately trained persons are at best illegal and can eventuate in homicide or suicide or both. The lives of innocent people, even totally uninvolved strangers, may be taken.

Also, this is not often accomplished in supermarket aisles or barnyards, even though Dr. Karl Menninger once remarked that psychotherapy could be practiced in a barn, and Dr. Viktor Frankl practiced analytic therapy in a Nazi death camp.

The key to personality change, apart from the inexplicable, is some form of transference psychotherapy which requires from 50 to 200 or more hours, almost always in an office, or on a hospital ward. In lay terms, transference involves the responsible, knowledged, risk-taking therapeutic handling of the transferring of a consultee's feelings, both positive and negative, from the rightful recipient in the dim past to the consultant in the present. Those who wish to undertake this kind of exhausting consultation should seek admission to the associations mentioned above, and be prepared for a lengthy, arduous, and costly pilgrimage. "For many are called, but few are chosen."

Relatively few people seek this kind of consultation. Those seriously desiring the competence to do this kind of work, having been forewarned, are also encouraged to proceed, since "The harvest is plentiful, but the laborers are few."

## 12. Escapism or Distraction

The most extraordinary prejudice concerning concepts I know of is that against "escapism." Being accused of seeking to "escape" responsibility, worry, reality, drudgery, etc. seems a vile charge in our achievement-oriented society, only slightly less criminal than malfeasance of office, misuse of public funds, or child molestation.

Actually, human beings have imperative need at times to escape intolerable good re : escape !

situations, impossible pains, severe crisis. Our physical bodies have the wisdom to impose escape at times—from mild fainting spells to potentially lethal heart attacks which force us to escape. The military services have learned through deadly experience the imperative necessity for "R & R" (rest and recuperation). The entertainment industry—from nomadic spell-weavers around primitive campfires to multimillion-dollar media extravaganzas—is founded on the human need for periodic escape. At times the forms of escapism have been cruel and inhuman. ("Bread and circuses"—i.e. gladiatorial fights—kept the Roman Empire an empire for quite some time.) Religious festivals, retreats, the hearing of Bible stories and romantic tales of the Crusades, all provided needed escape from the drab daily existence of feudal serfdom. Such specific escapes as the arts, from the ceiling of the Sistine Chapel to black spirituals, have done the same.

There are times when what people most desperately need is not confrontation, combat, one more straw added to their overburdened spiritual or mental backs. There are times when "getting away from it all" provides the time and means for reorganization in order to re-accept responsibility. This is what mental hospitals ("psychotic episodes") are all about. (We used to call such places asylums—places where the totally overburdened, whose mental and emotional circuits were drastically overloaded—could gain, for a time, respite, asylum, in order to be able to restore.) Recreation is just that—re-creation.

The evening after I had my first possible myocardial infarction, I was taken to an All-Star football game by some good neighbors. By halftime I'd forgotten the vial of pills prescribed by the emergency room physician. For the moment, I had escaped. Later I came back to resolve the unsolvable problems created by the confusing conflicts that ensued the destruction of our home by a massive tornado and the thousand personal crises that followed. It was an exciting ball game and I cannot recall who won on the gridiron, but I know *I* won, because I was able to escape.

My graduate thesis was based on two years of conversations with people suffering from acute and chronic "schizophrenic reaction, paranoid type" disorders. Assisting them to be distracted, to escape the torments of their lives (half of the "subjects" were incarcerated in what used to be called the "Criminally Insane Ward," a maximum-security facility) was a major step in their eventual rehabilitation. (Regrettably for a number of them, "rehabilitation" meant getting them into sufficient shape to stand trial for murder.) Nevertheless, the point is that sometimes people need distraction, to escape.

Any person who is on the way to the bridge, who is carrying a loaded gun, who has stockpiled poisons, or sharpened an ax, and who really needs distraction or escape, has a right to expect help of that kind from a consultant.

There may be a lot more consultation needed later, but in severe crisis, people deserve at least that to begin with.

30

Those of us whose situations are less dramatic may also deserve a little escape. The following segments of several conversations in a public restaurant illustrate this principle:

"That will be $2.10 for your lunch."

"I have the exact change."

"Thank goodness something has gone right at last. We're out of dimes."

"You look beat."

"Miserable would be more like it. Between Phil and the kids—don't ever let kids grow to be teenagers. I'm afraid I'm losing my mind. I haven't been happy since I was fourteen and read *Wuthering Heights.*"

"Could I help?"

"Give me something good to read."

"I have a new gothic novel with me. I got it this afternoon and won't get to it until the weekend. You're welcome to it."

(Two days later)

"I missed you yesterday. Your replacement had plenty of dimes, however."

"I started that book when I got everyone to bed. I read until three A.M. I called in sick yesterday and finished the book. It was a good rainy day to stay in bed and read. Here's your book. I feel great. Phil is going to talk with the school counselor this afternoon, and he's taking ME out to dinner tonight after this place closes.

"I think I'll go by the library and get another book by that woman. I really feel great. Hope your lunch is good."

A transactionalist would say the consultant had given her permission to escape, to become distracted, to get restored. She's done fine ever since.

Have you gone fishing, seen a football game, read a romantic novel, built a model, painted a picture, built a grandmother clock, watched a B television program, attended the opera, written a chapter of your life story, dined out, taken a nap, played golf, listened to country music, taken a piano lesson, read a catalog, played chess, or done as you irresponsibly damn-well pleased lately, to "get away from it all"? If not—if not regularly, I know a good emergency room specialist I can recommend—before it's too late.

Sometimes we need escape, distraction.

*part II*
Secret Meanings
in
Spoken Messages

## Introduction to Part II

The opening section of this book stressed finding out what people are asking of us before we provide help. The point of that section is that we most effectively help others when we know what they want and need. This may seem a very simple matter. Finding out what others want, however, is not always done quickly and easily.

One reason why we may have difficulty determining what people are asking of us is that people often conceal from themselves and others what they need. People may be afraid of or embarrassed by their true feelings and unmet needs, hence they protect themselves. This causes problems when the consultant seeks to know what troubles people.

Consultants also have "concealment devices" which may interfere with accurate perception of what others are asking. Some areas of need may threaten us, so we are slow to recognize them in others. We may even unconsciously assist the person in not realizing upsetting insights.

Part II of this book demonstrates how we can recognize and work through some of these problems that interfere with communication. Samples and examples of the "secret meanings" that are concealed in spoken messages are given as guides for the consultant. These should remove much of the mystery or confusion that routinely crops up in pastoral conversations. These guides will enable you to simplify your perceptions of people. You can then communicate with people more clearly and comfortably. This will give you greater confidence as you consult.

## 13. Ascertaining What We're up Against

If your desire is to help anyone anywhere, you need to know what we're up against. The desire to help is so innocent it seems, the concept so simple —how could we be "up against" anything.

We are up against ourselves. Our own blind spots, our lack of courage, conviction, common sense, concentration, and competence all work against us.

We are up against the parts of personality in others that resist recognition, resent information, ignore advice, avoid catharsis, reject feedback, abhor change.

We are up against the "threat of power" and the "violence of love."

We are up against weariness with well-doing, boredom with the pettiness of human nature, the temptations of knowledge, the corruptions of power.

The following sections are designed to lay bare that which we are "up against." Irritating suggestions as to what we or others are *really* communicating are pointed out in seemingly simplistic fashion. The major stereotypes of human relationships are outlined with an embarrassing lack of sentimentality.

You need guts to read the following pages, put the controversial concepts contained in them to the clinical test, and then decide whether this book is for you or not.

You will learn that you will no longer be able to talk the way most of us talk, that "normal" communication is a cop out, that you've been kidding yourself, or have been allowing others to kid you for a long time.

But.

But, if you really want to help anyone anytime, you'll give some attention to the following, swallowing your prejudices against what I have written, and making a final decision on the basis of honestly tested experience—with others —and with yourself.

If.

If you really want to help anyone anywhere, you need to know what WE'RE up against.


## 14. Getting in Our Own Way

Everybody I know who has gone into ministry or any other helping profession does so from self-interest. I was afraid of life in general and people in particular. Early I learned to appease people, to "get along with" others, to avoid competition. Later I learned to find ways in which I could control *some* people—and I avoided the others. At length I discovered religion, the ministry, as a way of both getting along with *and* controlling others.

Pastoral care and counseling is really the best of all worlds when it comes to getting along with and controlling others. I got along with competition because most of my seminary classmates sought Doctorates in Something Else and I thought most of my counselees would be my inferiors in some way.

Oh, I played at the competition game. I was the best bench warmer on an all-star high school and an undefeated college football team. I won speech contests and was the best debater in the league. I was elected to be president of almost everything from the senior high class to the State Chaplains' Association.

But underneath it all, I kept getting in my own way. I have an "at leaster's" script (see section 22) so I answered in the affirmative when a committee person at the "national level" asked me, "Do you feel that if you can help people, you'll have greater self-confidence and a firmer self-concept or identity —be helped yourself?"

After that I got down to business. I no longer get in my own way quite so often.

You probably know what it is about you that gets in your way when you _try_ (see section 18) to help people. Do you always have to be right? That will get in your way "every time you go through a doorway." Are you insistent on being the most humble person around? The most virtuous? Most helpful? Most pious? Most?

Does your self-esteem depend on being helpful? I used to have terrible trouble growing anything. I was the original "brown thumb." All my plants died. An expert was consulted. I helped my plants too much. They needed to be talked to, not lectured endlessly. Watered, not drowned. Fertilized, not buried in the stuff, burned up with it.

People are that way. "Smother love" is not limited to mothers. Consultants can catch it too. If you try to do more than is asked of you, people will cross the street when they see you coming.

What about being too nice? I love to be nice to people. Once, in the "snake pit"—the back ward of back wards of a state mental hospital—I was very very nice to a very, very "crude" patient. She vomited on me. Too much sweetness makes anyone nauseous.

Do you feel driven to get to know people intimately? Getting too close emotionally can make people very anxious. More crimes are wrought by closeness than this world dreams of. Don't be a victim of your need to get too close! (See section 24.)

Insisting on perfection can get in one's way. My mother taught me that "if a thing is worth doing, it's worth doing poorly," and that "half a loaf is better than none." If people ask your recognition, or advice, and you insist on a complete personality transformation, you'll get in your own way every time —not their way, since they'll be long gone.

36

There are a number of clues to the ways in which we can get in our own way. Some are suggested in sections 15–23. A major question we each need to ask of ourselves generally, and with each person to whom we provide help, must be: How do I go about not getting what I want? How do I avoid attaining the goal for which I set out?

I talked recently with a person with whom I have "communication problems." The conversation was far from satisfactory. I reviewed my typical behavior when I am in this person's company and learned the following: I avoid mutually satisfactory communications with this person by

a) doing most of the talking
b) losing my patience
c) trying to force my will on the other person
d) deciding before the person finishes speaking what is going to be said and responding to that, rather than hearing the person out
e) speaking before thinking
f) taking myself too seriously, the other person not seriously enough.

Armed with this brief list, I had another conversation with this person, avoiding these six behaviors. Communication was delightful. I have a new friend with whom I am comfortable.

Most of us know how we avoid getting what we want. The question is incredibly easy to answer. But without such awareness called to mind consciously, we will have disappointing results in helping anyone anywhere.

## 15. Nonverbal Communication

So many volumes have been written about nonverbal communication that this section may be an insult to readers. The standard classic in this field, seldom read, but essential, is *The Psychopathology of Everyday Life* by Sigmund Freud. All later works are but extensions of the basics outlined there.

Clenched fists, obscene hand gestures, heads shaking "no" while lips say "yes," kicking feet, forgotten names, slips of the tongue, crossed legs, pinched noses, eyes shifting toward the door, arms folded across the abdomen, and too many more examples for this book all have meaning.

Laughter is a special form of nonverbal communication. Most who read this will be familiar with the standard theories that much of humor is disguised hostility—from the "mother-in-law joke" to the awful popularity of ethnic put-downs. That the True Clown is a mirror of the ultimate sadness within us all is also widely recognized.

Significant laughter also to be noted in consultation is laughter people direct at themselves when they report suffering, failure, or tragedy. Much entertainment value is ascribed to reformed alcoholics who are able to laugh at themselves when they "fall off the wagon," small businesspersons who joke about their most recent receiverships, and people who can join painful guffaws about multiple divorces.

Transactional analytic colloquialisms for such laughter include the "witch laugh" and the "gallows laugh." These terms refer to the laughter that accompanies defeats, disappointments, even deaths.

The paradigm for such "transactions" is the small child, struggling to learn to walk. Encouraging comments are forthcoming from assembled family. When the child stumbles, giggles burst forth, and when the child falls flat, there is a great burst of glee. Hugging and approval follow rapidly. The child is "conditioned," as the behaviorists might say, to entertain significant others by tottering, and receives rewards and affection for each failure. Later in life he or she usually recounts more serious failings and fallings with the echo "hee-hee" or "ha-ha."

When the consultant hears the witch laugh, she or he realizes that to help is to go against the rewards and appreciation of the consultee's entire family. We are up against heavy odds.

The important thing to realize is that one can seldom assume the meaning of nonverbal communications in the abstract. Each person has some unique meaning for every gesture, posture, mannerism, and movement or lack of movement.

"I wonder what it might mean that you tap your fingers on the counter?" is more rewarding than "You must wish I'd hurry what I'm saying—that's why you're tapping your fingers on the counter!"

When given the opportunity, people can usually communicate verbally what their nonverbal communications mean. When "told" what they mean, even if the "guess" is a highly educated one, people usually resent and resist.

Often raising the question of nonverbal meanings also raises anxiety to the point that communication diminishes. For this reason, I seldom report my observations of nonverbal behavior directly. I do note and record in my thoughts what may be communicated, then listen for confirmation of what I first suspected from looking.

Sometimes I put my hunches about nonverbal communication to a verbal test. "I'm not sure why, but as we talk I keep feeling as if we are about to discuss sex. Is this possible?" If my observations are accurate, the response may confirm the observation quickly—"Well, that is a problem I've been wondering about—why sex seems sooo important to everyone these days." No need to embarrass people in supermarket aisles by pointing out erotic behavior until one is asked to do so. (See section 26.)

The most effective consultation occurs when the "expert" does not race ahead of the consultee. Surely one who has a degree of clinical experience can

38

"tell the story" better than the consultee. Most experts have memorized the "stages" of marital disintegration and the steps in the "grief process." Reciting these to people caught in the painful exasperations of either frightens, confuses, even condemns people to "follow the plan." The wise consultant develops the patience to "stay with" the consultee, hence maintain helpful communication.

No area of consultation poses greater hazards of leaving the consultee behind and bewildered than the area of nonverbal communication. We all tell far more by our actions than we are ready to tell by our words. To have such unintended communications reflected back to us before we are prepared hinders our progress. There are times when this must be done (see sections 26 and 32). For the most part, however, the helpful consultant will receive nonverbal communications and only "use" them at the right time and in the right way for maximum help to the consultee.

## 16. The "Confused-Reluctant" Response

Earlier I stressed the imperative step of discovering what people are asking. The most frustrating phase of any consultation is the response one almost invariably gets when this or some other *significant* question is posed. Almost always the initial response is some variation of "I don't know."

People avoid the painful (sometimes) but rewarding (almost always) "work" of improving their lot in life or way of life. Changing from the familiar to the unknown is always anxiety-producing. We are creatures of habit, however miserable our habits may make us for twenty or fifty years. Our first response to the possibility of a different (better) way of being is to draw back, to be fearful, confused, and reluctant. Or, as the saying goes, we prefer familiar hells to unfamiliar heavens.

Rather than be frustrated by such a response, the experienced consultant realizes that he or she has "hit pay dirt"—asked the right question at the right time, gotten to the growing edge, which is always threatening.

The wise consultant will not be confounded by the confused-reluctant response. She or he will give the consultee a moment or two, muttering something like, "humm-ah-humm." Then in a quiet but firm voice the consultant will repeat the question, expecting a second, more amplified "confused-reluctant" reply. The consultant will provide as much time as is reasonable under the circumstances for this second avoidance. Then, very matter-of-factly, the question is asked a third time with just enough "coldness" of tone to communicate that such repeated nonsense will not be tolerated.

The consultee will then answer the question or begin working toward answering the questions. At times the question should be assigned as homework for the next meeting when the consultation is terminated.

*get through the defensive confusion*

The following verbatim account of an actual supermarket aisle consultation will be a rough approximation of all the confused-reluctant conversations you will experience with almost anyone anywhere.

"Say, Reverend, I maybe ought to talk to you. I *may* have a problem, ha ha."

"Sure. What would you like to do?"

"Tee-hee-hee. You'll probably think I'm nuts or something. I mean whenever I try to talk with my husband about this, or anything for that matter, he just says to quit worrying. Like with the kids. You know one of them, the middle one, we had to the psychologist. Child psychologist, he called himself. Well, he saw Neddy twice. Just twice. I was so mad at that man. He was supposed to be an expert. Well, I've had my fill of experts. Don't you think a lot of experts have too much book-learnin' but no common sense? My mother always said common sense was hard to find as snowflakes in August. Now there is a woman with a lot of common sense. Not like my dad. I guess Dad has sense of one kind or another, but he never knew anything about kids. Still doesn't. If you got nearly killed he'd say not to worry about it. You didn't dare cross him. He was *always* right, no matter what. Mom was always so full of common sense. I don't know but what I am nutsy. What do you think? Ha ha! [pause]"

"Well, I think I'm not sure what it is you are asking of me. Tell me how I might be of help."

"Ha! You tell me! You're the expert. That's the trouble with everybody. When you need help, everyone expects you to do all the work yourself. I mean, I know I can't expect you to solve all my problems. My husband's OK I guess, usually. But he just doesn't . . . Oh, I don't know. I don't know what to do. I thought that if I talked with someone, like you, you know, maybe that you could, I mean, people are supposed to talk to their ministers, aren't they? I mean people do, don't they? [pause]"

"Umm. [pause, thoughtful look for a moment] Now tell me what you're asking from me."

"I knew you'd ask me that question. Oh, I don't know for sure. I get confused. I guess I just want someone to talk to, to listen to me. Does that make sense? I mean—"

"[Interrupting] Yes. You want to tell me what's troubling you, confusing you?"

"I knew you'd understand. [pause]"

"You look as if you're about to cry."

"[Gulps] No. I'm all right. What worries me most is etc., etc."

40

## 17. Declarations and Certain "If" and "You" Statements

Probably the most important statements to note are the early "Declarations" people make when seeking consultation. By Declaration I mean a rather adamant statement, usually uttered by the consultee with an attitude of confidence that we will agree without question. The Declaration is an assumption presumed not to be debatable or even questionable. Declarations sound very common-sensy and are usually presented as a preamble, a kind of introduction to any serious consultation. They are actually poisonous, sinister warnings and tell a volume about what we're up against.

A common Declaration runs like this: "I know that no one can solve my problems but myself, and if you etc. etc." The tendency is to listen to the "etc. etc." and ignore the Declaration. The Declaration is what we're up against— an adamant statement warning us that the consultee does not believe we can solve her or his problem. The Declaration is a denial of the efficacy of our craft, a prejudgment that whatever we provide will be useless at best, a waste of both our time at worst. The very common-sensy nature of the Declaration tempts us not even to notice, let alone question, its glaring assumption.

Common sense, however—True Common Sense—questions the Declaration immediately. What garbage! No one can solve your problem? That's what I'm in business for! If I can't solve your problem you really are wasting our time—unless you have something else in mind—like Dumping. I may be quite willing to be Dumped on, but don't preface your Dumping with such a stupid Declaration. The reason you're Dumping is because you of all people have NOT been able to solve your problem. And I can—if you ask me to, want me to. Or if I can't, I'll bet I know someone who can!

Of course, we would not say such things out loud, not right then, but we do note the Declaration and realize what we're up against.

Other typical Declarations include: "I know nothing can be done with teenagers!" "Nobody could understand how I feel!" "Nobody can change the way we are!" "We all must bear our cross!" And so on.

The important thing to do is note the Declaration and realize that is what we're up against. This will avoid surprise and disappointment later when the Declaration's power becomes evident.

Certain "if" statements can give hints as to what we're up against. I recall a statement I made many years ago that included the seemingly innocuous "if." After several years of financial struggle personally, I was surprised with a salary increase that added almost 40% to my anticipated income. I said, gloating over coffee, to a colleague, "If I don't start living on Easy Street soon, something is bound to be radically wrong!" Within six months I had worse financial woes than ever. The important part of my statement was "something is radically wrong!" The "if" part was merely a smoke screen or disguise for the truth of the matter—something *was* radically wrong with my personal financial practices.

When someone uses the "if" in a prefixing clause, note the weighty substance in the suffix. That will tell you what is *really* going on. Examples of this include:

"If I don't use the information my doctor gave me wisely, then I'll end up with another unwanted pregnancy."

"If I haven't learned my lesson by now, I'll deserve to go to prison."

"I now know that if I don't straighten up and fly right, I'll lose my family as well as my self-respect."

"If I take just one drink, I'll end up on skid row."

The transactional analysts have taught us the powerful meaning of "you" statements. They have pointed out that "when the client speaks in the second person, he or she is quoting someone." Usually that someone is a parent, perhaps a grandparent, who has indoctrinated the person with a philosophy or attitude toward life that is usually detrimental to the happiness or even the health of the client.

I recall a slogan I often heard at home—"You can't win them all!" When our high school football team won nine regular and three postseason games, the final one being the Thanksgiving Day State Championship, I realized that "You can't win them all" is not true. I know that such slogans and messages are designed to protect the young from disappointment and hurt if they do not "win them all," and may have their roots in the best of good intentions. The result can often be a stultifying of the zeal of youth, a "witch message" that places a "curse" of failure and defeat on those who accept such lessons as blueprints for mediocrity.

The experienced consultant wil note "you" messages as another means of recognizing what we're up against. Typical "you" statements follow:

"You have to accept the bitter with the sweet."

"You can't win!"

"You never know what's going to happen."

"You can't get ahead."

"You can't fight City Hall." (Note: Together with two other ministers and two lay persons, I did once "fight City Hall" and from our efforts we succeeded in driving a national crime syndicate out of a community of over 30,000 people; entrenched corrupt public officials were ousted from office and punished by fines and imprisonment.)

"You'll never make a million."

"You never change."

42

## 18. The Word "Try"

There are two uses of the word "try." One is legitimate, honest, of little consequence to the consultant. Examples include statements such as, "I'll try on this coat to see if it fits," or, "She wants to try out for the cheerleading team."

The other use of the word "try" is at best self-deceptive, and often intentionally designed to be misleading to the hearer. In this second use, which is of considerable import to the consultant, the word "try" really means FAIL. The following are examples of this communication to which the Gestalt therapists alert us:

"Reverend, I'll try to be in church Sunday morning."

"Honest Honey, I'll try to stay sober through the whole party."

"Next month I'm going to try to make up the time I've missed on the job."

"I'll try not to charge another thing until we've paid off what we owe."

"I'll try to stop by early in the week to see how you're doing."

"I'll try to learn Latin."

"I'll try harder next time."

And so on. The important thing is mentally to substitute the word "fail" in each such sentence we hear. This will help us know what we're up against.

"The important thing is to try, correction—to *succeed* at taking note of such statements."

## 19. The Word "It"

Again we are indebted to Gestalt therapy for an understanding of the true meaning often concealed from the consultee and consultant when the word "it" is used.

"It," when used in the personal sense, translates "I" or "me." Substitute "I" or "me" for "it" in the following:

"It's very difficult these days."

"I can't understand it. It doesn't make sense."

"Sometimes I think it's just plain crazy."

"It takes a long, long time to grow to maturity."

"I can't explain it—you'll never be able to understand it all."

At times a slight reorganization of a sentence will be necessary. Examples include such statements as:

"It's not easy to stop drinking to excess." This is reorganized to "I cannot easily stop drinking to excess."

Again the thoughtful consultant will note such uses. Only at the "teachable moment" will the consultant point out that such a use of "it" is a way of not accepting responsibility. When we rephrase statements, changing "it" to "I" or "me," we acknowledge and accept our responsibility in the matter at hand.

## 20. The Word "Can't"

"Can't" means "won't" when used in the *personal* sense. Such *factual* comments as "I can't lift the Grand Canyon" or "You can't grow two feet taller after your thirty-sixth birthday" mean just what they say.

Personal statements, however, usually are best translated so that intentions rather than limitations are made clear by substituting "won't" for "can't."

"I can't win" means "I won't win" and reflects a despairing attitude toward the self that resists considerable challenge from the consultant.

"I can't communicate with my teenage children" indicates a fairly firm determination on the part of the speaker NOT to accept responsibility for not being open to suggestions that might facilitate communication.

"I can't understand why people want to mongrelize the races" suggests stubborn resistance to any open-mindedness to increased sensitivity in racial relations.

"I can't let you solve all my problems for me" means "I won't let anyone help me."

"I can't handle money responsibly."

"I can't quit running around."

"I can't do anything right."

And so on.

Pointing out this interpretation of "can't" is a delicate matter since people usually resent such penetration of their defenses. When a consulting relationship is so structured as to permit explaining and asking for compliance with the theory that "can't means won't," the consultant had best be armed with ready suggestions as to how the "can't/won't" could become a "can/will." The following is an example.

A middle-aged woman was bemoaning the fact that she had experienced an unhappy and deprived adolescence.

"I was too inhibited by my mother. I never got to go to dances at school, was forbidden to date, not allowed to go on hayrides. I had to listen to classical music—popular music like the other kids liked was not permitted. I never had sweaters and skirts—always dresses, very proper dresses. Hamburgers and Cokes and hot dogs were considered junk and I was only allowed to eat boiled vegetables. I used to think french fried potatoes were worse than people think hard drugs are now. I missed the senior prom, football games, movies, every-thing a teenager is supposed to experience.

"I can't make up for that."

"You mean you *won't* make up for those things you missed?"

"NO! I mean I can't! Those opportunities are gone forever."

"You mean you WON'T. You can, you know."

"Tell me how, wise guy. How can I be a teenager again?"

"Oh, you can't become a teenager again—but you can enjoy the kinds of experiences you missed out on then—make up lost ground, so to speak."

"As I said before, wise guy, how?"

"There are dance studios and a square-dance club in town. The church youth group always needs chaperons for hayrides and wiener roasts. You can turn on any kind of music you like on the radio, and even buy albums of music from any decade—your mother is not around to criticize. You can afford to dress in any style you wish—and this is the age when 'anything goes' dress-wise. You can eat any way you like. You can't go to the senior prom but the Women's League Charity Ball is about the same thing every year. You even know the chairperson this year so you know you can get tickets. They'll sell season tickets to the local high school football games, and movies are available —from current hits in the suburban theaters to all the oldies you missed back then. You can do those things, have those experiences now."

"Oh, but I *couldn't*—I'm not the person I was then. I'm too shy—I'd feel like a fool."

"You mean you *wouldn't.* You could. You *are* the same person you were then—only now you say you are shy—then you said your mother inhibited you."

"Go to hell, Mr. Smart Alec!"

"I've changed my mind—you're not so shy or inhibited. In fact you come on pretty strong. How about using some of that strength to get into a square-dance club, buy a wardrobe, grill hamburgers, join a club—whatever."

"I guess I . . . *I could!*"


## 21. The Word "But"

Two theories exist as to the significance of the word "but" in the middle of a sentence—or other words such as "however" and "nevertheless" which may serve the same function.

One theory holds that "but" cancels the meaning of the statement prior to the "but" *and* the statement following the "but." Thus in the sentence "I would like to help her but she won't listen to a thing I say"—the statement

"I would like to help her" is canceled, and the statement "she won't listen to a thing I say" is canceled. The result is a seeming statement or couple of statements which actually mean nothing. A person uttering such a sentence usually does so with considerable feeling, seeming to communicate nonverbally as well as verbally something of significance. Actually, nothing has been said, no matter how fervently and eloquently it has not been said.

The other theory holds that the "but" cancels only *one* of the statements flanking the "but." The person, in this theory, actually is stating something following or preceding the "but." Thus, "I would like to help her, but she won't listen to a thing I say" does have meaning. The meaning is either "she won't listen to a thing I say," or "I would like to help her." The difficulty is in determining which of the two has meaning.

My experience indicates that at cne time or another either theory may be accurate. Following are a few typical "but" statements.

"I wish to hell I could balance my family budget, but I never will the way things are these days."

"I believe we should always proceed with complete honesty and openness. However, when in Rome do as the Romans do."

"I'd like to help you out, but I'm a little short on cash this month myself."

"I want to get along with my husband, but he's so unreasonable."

"I so hope to get out of this mess, but there just doesn't seem to be any solution I can live with ethically."

Without exploring further, one cannot determine whether, in each case, one part of the above pairs of statements is true or whether neither is true. For example, we do not know if the speaker in the first sentence *wants* to balance the budget or not. Also one cannot be sure the speaker will *not* do so should the economy improve. Further conversation is needed to isolate the statements and explore them separately. This is the case with each example. Only as each statement is discussed separately can true meanings be discerned.

## 22. "At Leasters"

Transactional analysts have taught us that there seem to be three kinds of people. There are *losers*—they end up in the morgue prematurely, in jails and prisons repeatedly, or on the "skid rows" of life. (Some "losers" seem to go down in grand style, supported by taxpayers, whereas others starve in cold dark rooms feeling isolated from even their God.)

A second kind of person is the *winner*. Winners, by TA definition, know their limitations, what they want in life within their limitations, and attain what they want. For example, the poorly coordinated boy who lacks physical stamina but wants desperately to be on the team and manages somehow to be a bench warmer through high school and small college, can enjoy the team photographs on his den wall and exchanging stories of hard practice sessions as much as the "almost perfect" athlete who wins the Heisman trophy. The girl, on the other hand, who wants to be a Hollywood star but lacks talent is as miserable as the Hollywood star who really wishes she had a Ph.D. in physics, but never got the chance to finish her B.S. because of contractual agreements she could not break with Cosmic Media.

I know of a man who is well on the way to making his third million (dollars) who wants to be liked. Each conversation I have with him involves a renewal of a "non-suicide contract." I know another man who thinks being rich would be fun, but really wants to be liked, who has kept his job through two company "financial retrenchments" because people love him. The latter is chronically borrowing "fifty until payday" but his idea of suicide is to have a heart attack while lovemaking at age 167. If you know your limitations and you have, within them, what you want, you are a winner and are probably a little embarrassed at realizing this.

Then there is the third kind of person—the *at leaster.* These are people who say things like:

"My business went under, but at least I'm not in prison."

"I'm out of work, but my in-laws fed us well last night, so at least I'm not hungry."

"I may not be one of the city's ten best-dressed women, but at least I look good in discount-store pantsuits."

"I don't have a dime in the bank, but at least my credit is good."

"My husband isn't very romantic, but at least he's home every night."

"There is no adventure, no gusto in my life, but at least I have a good murder mystery story to read tonight."

"I'm never going to be rich and famous, but at least we have the best-trimmed lawn in the suburb."

"We don't have a thing for the kids for Christmas, but at least the Salvation Army is seeing to it that we have a hot meal every twenty-fifth of December."

Dr. Eric Berne has recorded an interesting observation. He suggests that one can tell winners from losers within a few minutes of hearing them talk at parties, in consulting chambers, wherever. The winners know what they will do if they lose. Losers have no idea that they might lose, but brag at length about what they will do when they win.

This brings up the concept of "contingency plans." People who always have contingency plans in the backs of their minds seldom get into severe trouble of their own making. Simple examples include folk who always carry a raincoat and/or umbrella, flashlight, first-aid kit, fire extinguisher, etc., in their automobile. There are others who assume it will not rain, that they will be home before dark, not cut their fingers, or have the auto catch fire. I know of one man who always carries two or three small safety pins on his key ring.

47

He has never been embarrassed by ripped trousers, and has more than once "saved" women at social affairs from having to sit out dances or wear their evening coat because some critical link in their garments separated unexpectedly. On my own key ring I carry a small screwdriver, miniature pliers, and an adjustable wrench. People laugh at this practice—until they need a splinter removed, a screw tightened on their typewriter, or a nut secured on their bicycle hand-brake lever. Then they ask where I acquired such handy implements.

The lack of having a contingency plan assumes more sinister proportions when boating without adequate life preservers, keeping loaded guns in desk drawers, or powerful medicines in cabinets small children can reach.

No doubt this section of this book sounds like a lecture from a Child Scout leader, but not being prepared for alternative courses of action, should our "best-laid schemes" go amiss, accounts for an amazing percentage of hospitalizations.

Therefore, one of the greatest services a consultant can provide consists of asking the question, "What are your alternatives?" or providing alternatives, as the suicide prevention clinics have been teaching us for years.

What would *you* do if . . .

She changes her mind?
The deal falls through?
The pension plan goes broke?
You can't get a baby-sitter?
You make a mistake in your checkbook a week before payday?
There is a tornado?
Your mother-in-law decides to *stay?*
You don't get admitted to The school?
You get fired from your job?
He dies?
(Other, specify)_____?

The significant point of all this is to realize that there really are three kinds of people. To impose our "winner's script" (or "loser's script") onto someone who really has settled on an "at leaster" approach to life is to ask for frustration.

The old adage runs "live and let live." Erikson's is more productive. Erikson says, "Let live!"

*This* is probably the most difficult lesson taught in this book. Not difficult in the sense of comprehension—but in practice. If you don't believe how difficult this lesson is, consider for a moment your spouse. Your children. Your parents. Your friends. Your parishioners. Do you "let live" whether they seem to be winning, losing, or at-leasting?

Winners in consultation learn and practice this lesson.

48

## 23. When Questions Are Not Questions

In a preceding section, attention was called to "Declarations" and their significance. At times questions are Declarations. Often the tip-off is the use of the word "why" in a seeming question. Consider the following rather typical question, which is not a question.

The scene is a suburban household. It is late afternoon. The (stereotype) homemaker and mother is in the kitchen putting the preparations for the evening meal in the refrigerator and oven. The husband enters from the carport. They embrace, both obviously glad to be together. Small-to-medium-sized children invade the kitchen shouting and shrieking of various injustices, needs, hurts, other demands for attention. The parents look at each other in resignation, giving up fantasies of quiet cocktails and a few moments of intimacy. With a heavy sigh one or the other shouts above the troublesome din the question which is not a question:

"Why can't you children go to your rooms or outside and play and let Mommy and Daddy have a few minutes to talk?"

In the minds of the parents, especially in the heat of battle, this may sound like an attempt to "clear the room," to get the children outside or upstairs so the parents can enjoy intimacy. Actually, if the wording is attended carefully, as children almost always do, the "question" is literally an invitation to a (loud and lengthy) debate as to *why* the children *do not* leave the parents in peace and quiet. The less literal, more dynamic actuality is that the "why" is politely ignored. The remainder of the sentence is respectfully appreciated as a request or command—"You children cannot go to your rooms or outside and play and let Mommy and Daddy have a few minutes to talk!"

The point is obvious. Questions are not always questions. They are very often disguised Declarations. Frequently heard examples include:

"Why do you have to get drunk every time we go out?"

"Why can't I ever balance our budget?"

"Why is it that women don't like sex?"

"How come all the experts cannot figure out why teenagers cannot be controlled?"

"Why do you always have to ruin everything?"

"Why can't we ever get along?"

"Why won't you ever be reasonable?"

And so on.

An interesting footnote to the above is the theory that "why" questions almost always are basically angry in origin.

*part III*
Exploring
the Inner Worlds
of Others

## Introduction to Part III

The first section of this book emphasized the importance of knowing what people are asking. The simple yet significant process of finding out what people want and need was demonstrated.

Part II elaborated by theory and example ways by which communications get garbled. Guides for recognizing the underlying needs and wants of troubled people were suggested.

Now that you have read these pages, and practiced finding out what people want, you are ready for the exciting work of exploring the "inner worlds" of other people. I use the term "exciting" because this work has the potential for helping people at a level of depth you may not have believed possible. You will probably want to read through Part III once to get the overall feel of this section. You can then return to specific chapters to refresh your memory as you recognize the different ways people with whom you consult are relating.

This Part also gives specific ways in which the consultant can be most helpful to people with different "inner worlds." You will learn that you need *not* "treat everybody the same way." This means you will not rely on any single "school of psychotherapy," such as always being "client-centered," or "analytic," or whatever. You will learn the most effective ways of communicating and of working with people who are different. The importance of recognizing the differences in people is illustrated by the following:

An eminent seminary president told an incident from his days as student pastor in a rural parish. One Sunday evening, following the worship service, the church members lingered for talk. The major topic of conversation among them was the waywardness of youth. Considerable recitations came from a number of them about the inconsiderateness, strong-headedness, rebelliousness, and general depravity of young people, with examples from the newspapers and neighborhood.

Finally, one woman who had reared an only child announced that she felt the fault was with parents. "You all know how well my daughter turned out," she continued. "I just decided early to train her right. Whenever she didn't do what she was supposed to, she got punished. She learned to keep her things neat, did the dishes, helped out from when she was small. I was strict and it paid off."

At that, an aged farmer, father of ten now-grown children said, "Yup, *one* of mine was that way too."

The point is obvious. People are different. Each of us has a variety of ways whereby we may relate to others, to life, to God. Each of us also has a "favorite" or habitual mode of relating.

For example, each of us has the capacity to grieve, mourn, or be despondent. When we suffer significant loss—of a loved one, of prized possessions, position, status, job, whatever—it is appropriate that we experience despair. Some, however, tend to be more or less chronically despondent for large periods of time, even when there is no readily observable cause.

Again, each of us has the capacity to become suspicious, distrustful. When strangers come to our door, especially when they introduce themselves with a too-cordial smile and a greeting such as, "I'm *not* selling anything," experience teaches us to become suspicious.

Each of us has developed a habit of adopting one mode of relating as a "favorite," most frequently or characteristically expressed. In any family there are those whose personalities are uniquely interfused with one particular mode of relating. In my own family, there is one member who somehow seems characteristically more dependent than others. Another is chronically crabby. Another flirtatious, seductive to some degree in almost any circumstance. Still another is skillfully and artfully capable of "working" people, using people in an opportunistic and manipulative manner. I like to think of myself as the brooding, depressed, put-upon member of the family. *They* think I'm always suspicious of everything and everyone. (No wonder I don't trust them!)

You could probably sort almost any family or congregation into such crude categories.

There are times when the habitual mode of relating becomes more than just the faintly recognizable "dominant theme" in the music of a person's life. At times the theme is played "triple forte"—so loudly that damage to the individual's life ensues, because almost all considerations of reality are drowned out by the massive, all-consuming surge of despair, suspicion, anger, etc. This condition is usually considered mental illness.

Competent consultants must be prepared to recognize these major modes of relating and know how most effectively to respond to individuals swamped by them. To ignore this reality in human relationships is at best to run the risk of hurting rather than helping. Far more severe consequences can eventuate.

The most common complaint or resistance to accepting and actively adopting this idea that people are different in specific ways usually takes the form of, "I don't like labels!" or "Pigeonholing is for the birds."

The only effective antidote to such irresponsible sloganizing is careful consultation by the would-be consultant with a recognized and competent consultant to discover her or his own major mode of relating. Psychotherapy and/or clinical training is usually the best method of attaining such insight. Once a consultant knows about himself or herself, he or she is able to notice the differences in others, and respond appropriately and helpfully.

## 24. Anger

The most common disruptive emotion the consultant encounters is anger. Therefore, a detailed religious, psychological, and *physiological* knowledge of anger is essential to competent consultation with the angry.

Since earliest times anger has been a concern to religious people. Primitive rituals frequently centered on the problems caused by the anger of people or of the gods. Anger was the emotion attributed to Cain when he invited his brother to go with him into that field. Anger separated Esau and Jacob. The brothers of Joseph sold him into slavery because of anger. Moses, in anger, smashed the tablets containing the Law. Saul threw a spear at David. Jesus looked at those gathered in the synagogue with anger. And so on.

In our own time we continue to be concerned with anger because, as in Biblical times, there is still a lot of anger felt and expressed. Anger exists not just in Vietnam, Beirut, South Africa, between Arabs and Israelis, among striking miners, or in university and ghetto riots, but in our churches and in our homes and in the privacy of our own thoughts.

The Biblical attitude toward anger is quite realistic. On the one hand, anger is recognized as potentially destructive. Admonitions directed toward the control of anger are recorded: "A soft answer turns away wrath" (Prov. 15:1) and "do not let the sun go down on your anger." (Eph. 4:26) On the other hand, anger is recognized as a normal human emotion: "Be angry but do not sin" (Eph. 4:26), and even at times as a divine attribute: "God's wrath has come upon them at last!" (1 Thess. 2:16) God is, however, also pictured repeatedly as being "slow to anger," and Christians are encouraged to avoid angering either God or other people: "Fathers, do not provoke your children to anger." (Eph. 6:4)

The variety of ways in which anger is presented in the Bible makes it difficult for us who are Christians to have confidence in our attitudes toward this emotion whether the anger is our own or that of others. Studies of the shades of meanings of Biblical words require delicate, diligent discrimination, and recent emphasis on reevaluating our ethical understanding of Scripture compounds our confusion when we encounter anger.

The specialized discipline called psychology of religion, however, offers some understanding of the nature of anger, its causes, and what to do about it.

The dictionary says that anger is "a strong feeling of displeasure and usually of antagonism." There are really two major categories into which the causes of anger can be divided. First, there are the obvious, direct causes. We become angry at injustice, whether we experience it personally or see it on a broader social scale. If someone steals from us or unjustly destroys what is ours—be it property or reputation—then we naturally become angry. If we perceive fellow human beings being robbed or having their property or personhood destroyed by unjust aggression—be it international warfare or "gentlemen's agreement" prejudice—we get angry—with obvious reason.

Direct, obvious, injustice-induced anger is something we tend to accept as worthy and as a cause to be proud. It is even enjoyable at times. ("Boy, did I ever tell him off," we report gleefully.) From the psychological point of view, we are done a favor when someone or some group gives us opportunity for the venting of justified anger (or "righteous indignation," as we were taught to call it in former years). An occasion for getting justifiably angry gives us an opportunity to reassert our personhood, our Americanism, our Christian fortitude.

The uncomfortable fact about anger induced by injustice is that the more we know about the injustice the less easy it is for us to be righteously indignant. With facts also come perspective, greater understanding, less opportunity for excusable rage.

Much public anger was engendered recently by the destruction of facilities at a public amusement park by "teenage vandals" in a southern city. In their area, this amusement park was the one attraction through which everyone could find inexpensive enjoyment. Those vandals ruined their own playground. The park was closed permanently, and it was easy to become righteously indignant, angry with "them."

For those who later learned about some of "them," however, it became less easy to be justifiably angry. One of the vandals had been abandoned by his mother in his infancy, had never known a father, had been in a series of unofficial foster homes, and was cared for in crude, if not cruel, fashion. In exchange for money he had been taught to steal by a woman who worked in and lived over a slum bar. He had never had a new pair of shoes, had never had sheets on his bed, and had never been read to, prayed with, or lovingly cuddled. He suffered from nearsightedness, which was never corrected by glasses, and he was undernourished. He had been told repeatedly by school and court officials that he would "never amount to anything" and had consistently been punished by corporal means at home—not for disrespecting the property of others, but for not stealing more.

He was fourteen years old.

The punishment for his participation in vandalism was that he would be taken from the most stable security he had ever known—the woman in the bar—and lodged with strangers in an overcrowded, understaffed institution for juvenile offenders.

When the facts are known, it is less easy to be righteously angry at this young man. We can't let people tear up amusement parks, but it is difficult not

55

to temper our direct, obvious anger with sorrow for the boy and for the fact that we live in a society that permits boys to grow up in such poverty of material necessities and spiritual values.

One becomes tempted rather to get directly, righteously angry with our society for letting such things happen. But, again, as we learn the facts about our society, the anger may diminish and sorrow may ensue.

The second major category into which anger can be placed is that of the less obvious, less directly perceived causes. Here, anger runs the gamut from the normal maladjustments of everyday life to anger that is symptomatic of severe mental illness. There is a sprinkling of so-called unconscious anger in most of us. This kind of anger can be a continuous thing. Some people seem to feel chronically angry. Understanding the causes is the first step toward constructive consultation with such anger.

Chronic anger, or any anger that does not seem to have a direct cause or a cause that is appropriate in degree to the intensity of the anger, may have a *physiological* basis. Most of us realize that when we are hungry we tend to be more irritable than when our physical craving for food is satisfied. It is less irritating, ordinarily, for the waitress to be slow bringing the check than for her to be slow bringing the food. Also, when we have a headache or an upset stomach or a bad cold or poison ivy or sunburn or any other minor or major physical disorder, we tend to be more on edge, less understanding, tolerant, or gracious.

It is possible that continued feelings of anger, a chronically hostile attitude, may mean that there is something physically disordered in a person. Chronic infections or physical deficiencies may make a person angry all the time.

A widely discussed example of this fact was the Jack Ruby case of several years ago, when considerable attention was paid to "psychomotor" or "subconvulsive" forms of epilepsy. Neurologists tell us that some people, suffering from electrical discharge disorders of the brain, may actually have "temper tantrums" much as other persons may have convulsive seizures.

Christian educators especially, beginning with church school teachers, should be aware that consistent angry behavior by a child may indicate the need for medical examination, not sterner measures of discipline. It has been demonstrated that some "bad" children become "well behaved" children through the competent professional prescription of certain medications.

There are also *psychological* factors which may be at the root of anger. Generally, any situation which causes stress and discomfort to a person produces the unpleasant experience called anxiety. The human mind is marvelously created in such a way as to enable us to avoid the unpleasantness of anxiety. Anxiety is an extremely disturbing experience about which we can do nothing directly. Dr. Harry Stack Sullivan has pointed out that we can do something about anger—discharge it in fighting; but the only thing we can do about anxiety is suffer it, or change it into something we can do something about. Much chronic anger is the result of our minds' ability to change the discomfort of anxiety into anger so that we can do something.

What are some of the things that make us anxious, that may lead to chronic anger? The most obvious cause of anxiety is the experience of being rejected, ignored, or not taken seriously as a person.

In marriage counseling one frequently discovers that a cause of a couple's unhappiness is the "bad temper" of the wife (or husband). It usually develops that "the only time he (she) seems to notice me, to pay me any attention, is when I have one of my rage spells."

Many of our "angry young people" act out their anger, not so much in order to champion their causes, whatever they may be, but as a way of claiming attention in a busy world of tremendous size and complexity that does not take young people very seriously unless they make a lot of money quickly or resort to violence. Understanding this may explain why meeting the demands of militant groups may not resolve the problem, may not satisfy them. They may not want their demands met like a doled-out allowance, given in hopes they will go away. They may want to be taken seriously as persons.

On the other hand, anger may be a means of reacting to overindulgence. Young people who are overindulged may be treated or feel treated just as "unseriously" as young people who are deprived by obvious rejection. Too much attention, too much closeness emotionally, too much "help," may stifle an individual. Psychiatrists sometimes call this "smother love"—and fathers can be just as "smothering" as mothers. (So can church people.) The angry rebellion of the young may be an attempt to get free to try things on their own.

A young man's parents may have provided the money, preparatory education, and wardrobe for him to enter an excellent college. The boy, in angry rebellion, says he would rather join the army. The parents, when finally convinced that he is going to do this to them, may respond with something like, "Well, Father will go down to the recruiting office and talk with them about this." This usually precipitates further explosions of anger, more extreme bids for freedom. The tragedy is that often such young men would really rather go to college. But they want it to be their decision.

Youth has no sole claim to this kind of anger. Admission workers in mental hospitals see a lot of elderly people brought into the hospital by their middle-aged children who are distraught because the parents angrily refuse to be placed in retirement or nursing homes. A busy consultant sometimes feels that half of her or his professional time is spent with parents seeking help because they can't make their children follow their instructions; the other half of the consulting time is spent with children who can't make their parents do what the children want. A lot of anger usually splashes around in these family conflicts and the underlying fact may be that, despite the best of intentions, neither antagonist communicates taking the other seriously as a person.

A third cause of anxiety's being translated into anger is seen when one is working with young children and with church congregations. This is anger that masks a bid for controls when the person is getting anxious about the possibility of losing self-control. The typical example of this is the small child who throws temper tantrums at bedtime, when overly tired. The later the bedtime is postponed, the more likely the child is to explode with this kind of anger. Frequently, to avoid the further wrath of the child, parents permit him or her to remain up "a few more minutes" or "until this program is over." This leads the overly weary child to more angry behavior. The child demands a drink of water. When the water is brought, it is rejected because "that's sink water and you know I want refrigerator water." The child is literally crying to be put to bed. One mother, understanding the dynamic, insisted that the child must go to bed because "you are too tired and that is what is making you so angry." The child promptly shouted back, "Well, it's your fault for letting me get too tired," and kicked the mother. He was immediately put in bed forcibly. Sometimes one angry kick will accomplish more than a hundred angry whines.

Prison chaplains sometimes meet men who, having been afraid of losing self-control totally, committed some "angry" crime, got caught, and thus were sentenced to a place where walls and bars insure against total loss of control.

In the church tradition that things be done "decently and in order," we have a divinely inspired, built-in system for reassuring those whose anger represents their fear of losing control. The parliamentary procedures for the conduct of church sessions, congregations, and national assemblies effectively counteract almost anyone's fear of losing control. When voices are raised in anger and a meeting starts to fall apart, anxieties mount. Ordinarily it is not necessary to kick the moderator to get parliamentary order restored. But if nothing else succeeds, that most probably will. In any event, sometimes anger is an unconscious request for help in controlling oneself. Firmness, not brutality, is what is called for.

Some people suffer from having a low opinion of themselves. They do not feel that they amount to much or that they could ever have much influence over others; they feel that they have been denied essential qualities as persons. Such individuals are uncomfortable around others. It is as if the nearness of other people would take something away from them. Such people may actually have been "doormats" to others; they may have been abused, used, denied love. Their interpersonal caution may be based on real rather than imagined disappointments in life with people. These individuals may express their *desire for emotional distance* through anger. They may expect to be embarrassed, humiliated, hurt. Rather than wait for what they consider the inevitable, they may go on the offensive and execute the interpersonal equivalent of "You can't fire

58

me, I quit!" by angry actions and words. The fourteen-year-old boy described earlier may well be such a person. His brief experience has indicated that the world is hostile, rejecting, using him rather than loving him. He acts anti-socially because he doesn't believe, he hasn't been led to believe, that anyone could really care for him. Overtures of friendliness, concern, and love are new and untrustworthy experiences for him—"Why would people be nice to me unless they were setting me up to be used?" he thinks. He expects to be abused or rejected, so he precipitates the rejection with his antisocial actions.

Some deprived persons have little ability to become emotionally involved other than at the level of hostility. Such people grew up in an atmosphere in which strong feelings of love were not expressed; affection and tenderness were ridiculed as signs of weakness. The only strong emotion tolerated was ex-pressed by the hostile exchange of words or possibly physical blows. People who are products of such an environment have a narrow range of emotional experience. Conflict is the only interaction with other people that really has meaning for them. Loving endearments, kind deeds are like a foreign language that they can neither comprehend nor speak. Such persons may look for arguments—at work, school, or home—as the only way they can experience emotional stimulation and expression. When you clash with such an argument-picking, chronically angry individual, you become a "center of affection" for her or him, satisfying an emotional craving for meaningful relationship. When young people from this type of background marry, their relationship is de-scribed as a "conflict marriage" and causes unending concern to their neigh-bors who think shouting and throwing things a poor way to carry on a marriage. The substitution of anger for other emotions is indeed never fully satisfactory—and can be morbidly destructive—especially where there are children involved and where firearms are readily available.

A final cause of anxiety's being translated into anger may be called "sad-ness anxiety." Sadness is the painful emotion we experience when something or someone we cherish dies or is otherwise lost to us. Anger is less painful to us than sadness. In the normal grief that follows the death of a loved one, or in the sadness that is a reaction to the loss of anything significant, we may lapse into anger at times as a relief from the pain of sadness. People who work in hospitals know this and are not surprised when the relatives of a patient who has died manifest anger toward the hospital, nurses, doctor, chaplain, pastor, or church. Perhaps they find relief in this anger because it is an active emotion, allowing much expression but little inner reflection. Sadness, on the other hand, is a quiet, reflective experience, deep and penetratingly painful.

Anger often causes concern in marriage. A couple may begin to quarrel much of the time after the honeymoon is over. In time a ritual of angry exchange may almost replace the actions of endearment and love which char-acterized the early stage of marriage. What happens sometimes is that we carry

59

into marriage conscious and unconscious ideals and fantasies—dreams as to what the perfect spouse will be like. Little by little, the reality of who our spouse really is threatens to destroy our dreams. Sadness at losing, at giving up the dream, is painful. We quarrel to avoid the pain. In the long run, however, accepting and suffering through the sadness, giving up the unreal dream, frees us to fall more deeply in love with the person to whom we are wed. A couple may have to work through this "crisis of intimacy" periodically throughout life. The reward is worth the effort.

When Christians meet anger in themselves or others, there are a few practical suggestions that may help. In dealing with anger in others the consultant should:

Maintain calm, stable, but reasonable self-control. Do not panic or lose your own temper.

Be discreetly honest, admitting your irritation in a firm but not uncontrolled way. Say, "When you start shouting it frightens (or angers) me," not *"Don't* you shout at *me!"*

Always respect the other person and treat her or him as reasonably responsible. Take that person seriously. Laughing at or ignoring him or her can goad the person to new extremes of anger.

Give the other person the emotional distance that seems needed, and avoid pomposity or authoritarianism. Don't crowd the person into a corner, either physically or verbally.

On the other hand, avoid excessive passivity and extreme permissiveness —which may be interpreted by an angry person as her or his not being taken seriously.

Speak clearly, matter-of-factly, meaning what you say and demonstrating what you say if necessary. "I cannot continue this discussion if you are not going to follow the rules. Let's take a coffee break."

With a chronically angry person who threatens to become destructive, recourse to proper authorities—legal or medical—may be necessary. If the family physician or attorney cannot advise you how best to handle relationships with an excessively angry person, they can refer you to someone who can give such advice. In rare instances, calling the police may be the only alternative left.

What do you do when you encounter anger in yourself that troubles you?

Attempt to pinpoint the cause of your anger, by introspective thought ("Now, why did I get so angry at him really?"). This can be attempted as a form of prayer, often with beneficial results.

Talk the situation over with another consultant—friend, pastor, counselor, any person whose opinions you trust.

Get a routine physical checkup from the family doctor, being sure to mention your concern over anger.

In the church setting, if you feel wronged by someone, take seriously the prescription outlined in Matthew 18:15–17: " 'If your brother sins against you, go and tell him his fault, between you and him alone. If he listens to you, you have gained your brother. But if he does not listen, take one or two others along with you, that every word may be confirmed by the evidence of two or three witnesses. If he refuses to listen to them, tell it to the church; and if he refuses to listen even to the church, let him be to you as a Gentile and a tax collector.' " There are formal procedures whereby anger can be dealt with "decently and in order" in our church settings, and we should not be reluctant to employ them. Creative, disciplined handling of anger is better than isolated nursing of grudges both for the individual and for the church.

Finally, remind yourself often that anger is a part of being human. Even small children ("to such belongs the kingdom of heaven") get angry—so angry at times that they blurt out fearful, nasty things. We may become consumed with anger so that we get too angry to eat or sleep or think straight, so angry that we are tempted to do as Cain did. This too is part of being human. "No temptation has overtaken you that is not common to man." (1 Cor. 10:13)

As we learn to accept anger and to understand it, anger no longer is master of our fate. Rather, Jesus Christ who overcomes "all our enemies" continues as our Master who can, despite our anger,

> Reclothe us in our rightful mind,
> In purer lives . . . [his] service find,
> In deeper reverence, praise.

Comprehending and accepting the above leads to competence in consulting with angry persons.


## 25. Apathy

In our time, millions of Americans are seriously concerned about the burning issues of human relations. A smaller number are vigorously involved in these issues. Among those not so concerned or active are some who are simply avoiding responsibility. But there are others who are apathetic in a deeper sense. Spiritual apathy is found in suburban churches, the poverty-pocket community center, the wards of the mental hospital, and in the privacy of personal devotions.

Apathy has been defined as "want of feeling; lack of passion, emotion, or excitement; indifference to what appeals to feelings or interest." This concept is nothing new. The absence of strong feeling has been criticized or praised throughout history. The Old Testament abounds with mention of apathy. In the New Testament we read the forlorn prophecy, " 'And because wickedness is multiplied, most men's love will grow cold.' " (Matt. 24:12) This seemed fulfilled to the writer of the Revelation who said, "I know your works: you are neither cold not hot." (Rev. 3:15)

In some eras and cultures, apathy has been praised. The attitude of the Stoic philosopher Emperor Marcus Aurelius typified an ancient "heroic apathy." When informed of his son's death in battle, he said, "I never thought I had begotten an immortal." In the present day, adulation and emulation of apathy as a virtue is widespread among teenagers, whose repeated admonition is, "Don't lose your cool." In some Eastern religions, detachment is a goal to be attained.

For the most part, however, apathy has been considered a bad thing. Early medieval Christians described several categories of sin which were apparently expressions of spiritual apathy. They include "tepidity" (being lukewarm), and "acedia" (spiritual sloth).

Spiritual apathy is not confined to church organizations or individual religious people. It tends to spread through all relationships. A woman confided to her pastor, "It is not just the church services that leave me cold. I feel that way at home, with other people, with my husband."

To understand spiritual apathy in the church we must first explore some of the reasons why individual people become apathetic. One cause is discussed by Gibson Winter in his book *Love and Conflict.* He says that we develop an emotional detachment in response to our competitive society in which "one belongs only if he succeeds." In such an atmosphere of being valued only for performance, one "changes like a chameleon, adjusting his attitudes and hopes to fit each new group with which he deals." Winter aptly calls such a person a "shrinking man" whose "insides shrivel." Hope, aspiration, dream, strong feelings, all become excess baggage that slow one down in the "rat race" of success-oriented life. Virginia Satir, a recognized authority in marriage counseling, writes in *Conjoint Family Therapy* ([Palo Alto, CA: Science and Behavior Books, 1967], p. 23) that modern life "mechanized and de-personalized the work world, leaving the male feeling like a meaningless automation, laboring at tasks which were only a tiny part of a gigantic, incomprehensible, valueless, whole. It caused individual worth to be rated by income earned, leaving the female feeling down-graded because she did not receive wages for keeping house and rearing children."

Along with such external pressures, the mobility of Americans causes apathy. Laments a typical suburban pastor, "Just about the time we have a well trained session ready to do the work of the church, half of the session members get transferred by their companies." This continual uprooting teaches us to avoid having strong feelings about our neighborhood, city, or church. If we get attached emotionally, then move, we lose something meaningful and have to begin all over again somewhere else. Soon we're tired of investing our feelings, only to be wrenched away from the objects of our affections. We are a "lonely crowd" because we have no place to call home.

Another apathy-inducing factor is our growing realization of the bigness of the universe contrasted with the smallness of ourselves. As we look into the galaxies with space-age sight we ask anew the psalmist's question: "When I look at thy heavens, the work of thy fingers, the moon and the stars which thou hast established; what is man that thou art mindful of him, and the son of man that thou dost care for him?" (Ps. 8:3–4) We wonder if our life on this planet is but "the buzzing of gnats in the light of a billion suns."

Added to this technical sense of smallness, the population explosion further convinces us of our infinitesimal unimportance. We personally do not see how we can do anything to ease the burdens of the world's three billion people.

There are other, more personal causes of apathy. These include certain inner dynamics with which the psychologist and psychiatrist are familiar.

1. One, already intimated, is this: apathy is a protection of the self against being emotionally hurt. Permitting ourselves to feel strongly about something or someone makes us vulnerable to injury. To believe in and work for a cause is risky, because we may discover the cause not worth the belief and the work. To feel strongly about someone may bring pain, for that someone may not feel strongly about us; that someone may laugh at us or may leave us. The greater the love, the greater the loss when the love is ended.

In our world of self-seeking and advantage-taking, it is dangerous to commit oneself to anything or anyone. Our trust may be abused; our commitment may be taken advantage of. Generations of apathetic persons make popular such songs as "What Kind of Fool Am I?" Inside most of us there is a survival factor that resists our being hurt, abused, made a fool of—even "a fool for Christ." We become apathetic to avoid injury.

2. Another cause of apathy is our reluctance to hurt others. We hedge at declaring ourselves openly, because inwardly we fear we may disappoint others by not living up to the declaration. A lot is demanded in the marriage vows—"wilt thou have this woman to be thy wife, and wilt thou pledge thy troth to her, in all love and honor, in all duty and service, in all faith and tenderness, to live with her and cherish her, according to the ordinance of God in the holy bond of marriage?" We feel like saying, "I don't know," to such an eternally demanding declaration.

In marriage counseling one often hears the complaint, "My husband never tells me he loves me," or "My wife does not show affection toward me." Frequently the cause of such apathetic response from a marriage partner is deeply motivated by the fear that saying such things, disclosing affection, may hold out promise and hope that cannot always be fulfilled.

Some people do not attend church because they feel inside that they are not worthy, that to be active in the church is to play the hypocrite. Some fear church commitments because they fear that they will fail to fulfill the commitment. One man refused to pledge at the time of the Every Member Canvass. His reason: "I got in trouble a few years back by making a church pledge that I could not fulfill. Oh, they said it was all right, and that they understood, but I do not ever want to feel I have let God's people and church down like that again."

3. A third cause of apathy in personal relationships may be deeply submerged anger. A very common way of expressing indirect anger toward one's family, pastor, or anyone else, is to appear unmoved emotionally by them. "When she gets angry she just clams up. I'd rather be shouted at," reports a frustrated husband in a marriage counseling session. He is right. He would rather be shouted at—and that is why his wife does not shout. She is seeking not to please him, but to hurt him.

Some people are angry with God. Life, created by God, "is of few days and filled with trouble." Many people have suffered—because of prejudice, war, the apathy of others, disappointed dreams. Although no one can understand fully the mystery of pain, almost everyone has feelings about pain. Often those feelings, deeply unrecognized, may be feelings of anger toward the God who created things as they are. Few thoughtful Christians go through life without becoming angry toward God at one time or another. Being apathetic toward God may seem safer and saner than shaking one's fist at the storm or shouting at a drought.

4. Apathy is also a protection against losing control of oneself. There are people who fear both their anger and their affection, and fear that the two may become mixed if they do not hold both in check. Almost daily one reads homicide-suicide headlines of estranged couples who had set out to restore their love. In marriage counseling, one frequently hears the apathetic partner say, "I just can't let myself go. I know I should be more affectionate, but what if the other, violent side of my feelings comes forth?"

The fear of losing control can hinder people from accepting church responsibilities. Within many of us lurks the subconscious fear that if we rise to speak in the congregational meetings, we will become angry and begin to shout. Perhaps it is safer and saner to remain quiet and say nothing. It is even safer not to attend the meeting at all. Theologically, the church should be willing to accept all of a person, including her or his loss of control. But we church folk have a long tradition of doing things decently and in order. Shouting in the sanctuary is not encouraged.

Persons suffering from spiritual apathy have somehow come to believe that their feelings are best left unexpressed. They think their most positive feelings may be unappreciated at best, and their more negative feelings may draw criticism. Mixed as they are within most of us, we fear that our emotions may be uncontrollable once we begin to express them.

Apathy can be tragic. At its worst it characterizes major mental illness. In other cases it causes an inner despair reflected by such popular songs as Rodgers and Hammerstein's:

> *If I loved you,*
> *Words wouldn't come in an easy way—*
> *Round in circles I'd go.*
> *Longin' to tell you, but afraid and shy,*
> *I'd let my golden chances pass me by.*
>
> *Soon you'd leave me,*
> *Off you would go in the mist of day,*
> *Never, never to know*
> *How I loved you—*
> *If I loved you.* \*

Antoine de Saint Exupéry in *Wind, Sand and Stars* (New York: Harcourt Brace Jovanovich, 1968) gives a description of the apathy of minor airport employees as perceived by the romantic and dashing airplane pilot. The employees are preoccupied with "humble meditations upon illness, money, and shabby domestic cares." The pilot's thought response is:

> Old bureaucrat, my comrade, it is not you who are to blame. No one ever helped you to escape. You, like a termite, built your peace by blocking up with cement every chink and cranny through which the light might pierce. You rolled yourself up into a ball in your genteel security, in routine, in the stifling conventions of provincial life, raising a modest rampart against the winds and the tides and the stars. You have chosen not to be perturbed by great problems, having trouble enough to forget your own fate as man. You are not the dweller upon an errant planet and do not ask yourself questions to which there are no answers. . . . Nobody grasped you by the shoulder while there was still time. Now the clay of which you were shaped has dried and hardened, and naught in you will ever awaken the sleeping musician, the poet, the astronomer that possibly inhabited you in the beginning. . . . when night has fallen, I, delivered, shall read my course in the stars.
>
> [Used by permission of Harcourt Brace Jovanovich, Inc.]

Christ promised us more than obsession with illness, money, and shabby domestic cares. He promised us life abundant. Our question is, what do we do about apathy—in personal life, and in the church?

In pastoral consultation we employ certain rules for working with the apathetic person:

---

\*Copyright © 1945 Williamson Music, Inc. Publisher and manager of all rights—T. B. Harms Company. Used by permission.

65

1. Notice what the apathetic person does not mention—the areas of life one ordinarily talks about seriously, but which are absent from the conversations of the apathetic. These are the areas where real hurt or pain has occurred. Know that they are there, and be sensitive.

2. Do not focus considerable public attention on the shy and quiet, possibly apathetic, person against her or his wishes. Being stared at, placed in the limelight, can embarrass a very sensitive person. Instead, provide opportunities for people of various temperaments to take part in church activities. Attempting to force or push the apathetic into greater activity may drive them away.

3. Avoid excessive emotional demonstrations toward the apathetic person. Lavish emotionality heightens the contrast between how you seem to feel and his or her own lack of feeling, causing increased discomfort.

4. Do not demand that the apathetic person respond to you, the church, or Christ with strong emotion. For example, people who seldom take active part in church work but do send a check, may be doing all they emotionally can. Criticism and rejection of what has been done, repeated urging that more be done, does more harm than good.

5. Place a positive interpretation on what the apathetic person does do. If she or he attends church and sits in the last row, appreciate the attendance rather than urging the person to move up front. Sending a mailed reply thanking a person who contributes a check may do more to communicate the acceptance of Christ than a visit by the evangelism committee, with well-intentioned insistence that more be done.

At one counseling session, a young woman complained, "My parents gave me money and everything money could buy. But they never gave me love." In time she realized that her overworked wealthy father was giving her love the only way he could—through gifts. His own emotional background deprived him of the capacity for warmth and affection. Similarly, some apathetic people are unable to articulate or act out their Christian faith. The giving of gifts, even small ones, may be the only means of communication possible to them.

6. Always keep promises and be faithful. The apathetic person feels that she or he has little worth. If our promises to them are not kept, or faith is broken even in minor matters (such as not returning borrowed items, and failing to acknowledge small contributions), the apathetic person will suffer, and may interpret the oversight as a confirmation of his or her own lack of worth. Being prompt is also very important. If a consultant is late for an appointment with

such persons, they may believe that the consultant really didn't want to keep the appointment.

What does a person suffering from spiritual apathy do to counteract it himself or herself? There are several things that can help:

1. Realize that all of us have times of apathy. This is part of the price we pay for being human. It may seem sinful, but the church is made up of sinful people. Accepting who and what we are is a part of being accepted by God in Christ.

2. Admit to those we trust that we are apathetic. For every person who will chide us, there is another who will accept us. Neither God nor the church expects more of us than we are able to give. Admitting to a pastor or a nominating committee that we are not up to fulfilling their request is nothing of which to be ashamed. Truthfulness is not shameful, and it has a strange way of making us more able the next time we are asked to serve.

3. If apathy causes us to be consistently unhappy, to lose weight, sleep, or friends, it may indicate a medical rather than a spiritual cause. The family doctor or a psychiatrist can often be of more help in overcoming apathy than the self-recriminations of a decade.

4. The trust that apathy will not always be our lot can keep us going day by day, and can give us the courage to risk reaching out to God and to other people for help.

Finally, when spiritual apathy overcomes the church or the individual, we must remember the words of Paul (Rom. 8:39): nothing "will be able to separate us from the love of God in Christ Jesus our Lord," (not even our apathy), and the words of 1 John 3:20: "whenever our hearts condemn us . . . God is greater than our hearts, and he knows everything."

## 26. Eroticism

Some people seem to relate primarily at the erotic level. Consulting with them successfully requires (a) recognition of the overt and/or covert sexual character of their relating, (b) comprehending the variety of reasons people may adopt eroticism and sexual seductiveness as a prime mode of relating, (c) an awareness of one's own sexuality, and (d) knowing and implementing procedures in consultation that are helpful rather than harmful.

Eroticism may be heterosexual or homosexual. The following can be applied to either expression of sexuality.

A. We need to be aware of the various ways in which sexuality becomes the means of communication between others and ourselves.

1. Most of us recognize the sexy nature of clothing some people choose to wear —tight garments, revealing attire, and seemingly "accidental" characteristics of dress. An example of the last is the woman who habitually seems to have forgotten to button her blouse completely, or the man who did not get his zipper closed all the way. This leads to the old joke about the girl who had nine buttons but could only "fascinate." The way jewelry is worn can be quite erotically designed to call attention to breasts, hips, ankles, etc. The ordinarily slovenly person who dresses up for certain persons such as the consultant may be communicating a selective seductiveness by manner of dress.

2. Conduct can be seductive. Sexy posing, the flexing of muscles, straightening hose, offering to show "the scar from my operation," and other exhibitionistic behavior is usually noted by the alert consultant. Seductive behavior can be subtle. The giving of gifts and the doing or asking of favors can be erotic expressions.

Any "softening-up" technique can be seductive. The traditional female expression of this is tearfulness which usually "hooks the nurturing Parent" of the consultant, causing him or her to want to embrace the consultee, initially as one embraces a weeping child to comfort. Other emotions can thence take over or be communicated unintentionally. The classic homosexual "softening-up" approach is to begin to exchange jokes, first of a mildly sexual nature, progressing to the stimulating "hardcore pornographic" level, then switching to serious talk at the philosophical or gutter level, about the need for broadmindedness about free love.

Perhaps the most subtle seductive behavior has been elaborated by Bennett Cerf, who in response to a survey question "What is sex appeal?" replied, "When a girl looks at me as if I had sex appeal, then *that* girl has sex appeal!!" Clergy and others who frequently address groups from pulpit or lecture-stand almost always note a few such people during the first few minutes of facing the crowd.

3. The way people "structure" a relationship may be seductive. Examples include the person who wants to consult in romantic rather than readily available space—who indicates she or he would feel more comfortable talking in a candlelit cocktail lounge or the nearby park than in the store or "stuffy office." Inviting the consultant over to the apartment for a meal, to the comfort of the hayloft, or suggesting a quiet drive down a rural lane all carry overtones of seduction.

"Accidental" structuring may be more subtle. For example, repeated "surprise" meetings of the consultee with the consultant at unexpected places at

68

propitious moments may be neither accidental nor surprising in retrospect. One pastor, responsible for appointing church members to a variety of committees, became aware that a certain attractive young woman kept showing up for committee meeting after committee meeting, causing him to examine his own "unconscious" processes of selecting "a wide number of people from the church to fill these committees."

4. Conversation is the most common form of seductive behavior among the highly articulate. Sexy conversation can be veiled and includes talking about body parts, double-meaning statements, and discussing sex from the sociological, philosophical, or psychological standpoint. Lavish compliments including the never-fail stock statement "You are the *only* one who understands" are almost always erotic to some degree. Seductive conversation can also be overt. Open propositions and statements such as "I want to sleep with you" or "I love you" are obvious.

5. A consultee's dreams also may communicate an erotic attraction. A typical example is the consultee who wants to tell a puzzling dream. Somewhere in the dream some kind of physical sexual behavior takes place, "but I could not tell who the other person was. He/she was always in the shadows so I could not see the face. About your height, however. I wonder what that means?"

B. Eroticism can be placed in two major categories, which often overlap.

1. One is the category in which the erotically relating person is aware in full consciousness of what she or he is doing. These include the socially acceptable erotic behavior between a married or dating couple as well as the healthy flirtation that goes on among single people after the onset of adolescence.

There are also conscious seductive behaviors which border on the ethically questionable, such as those common in the political, advertising, and selling world. There, attractive young women in scanty garb are employed to solicit votes, cause us to remember the name of a particular brand of cigarettes or automobile tires, or handsome "touch-of-gray" late-middle-aged men dressed as airline pilots urge teenagers to purchase chewing gum that has no sugar and won't stick to their teeth.

The more traditionally recognized sexual conduct, from the merely frowned-upon behavior of prostitutes to the outright illegal and immoral acts of sex criminals, may include full awareness by all concerned of what is going on.

Most people are aware of having what Eric Berne calls a "front room" and a "back room" in their minds. The "front room" is the Victorian parlor in which everything is respectable. The "back room" is the bathroom, bedroom, or basement where things are kept "behind closed doors" so the neighbors won't know what is going on in that part of the mind. The small-town barber shop with hunting magazines and "fish-and-wildlife" or automobile racing calendar art in the front room always has a curtain separating the space young mothers can occupy while getting their children's hair cut from the space in which lewd photographs, whiskey, and games of chance exist. Most of us are aware of these separations in our minds.

2. The erotic behavior of persons is often an overt vehicle for their dimly perceived inner needs. Such can range from the benign to the catastrophic, personally and socially. The dynamics of "out-of-awareness" eroticism include:

a. *An appeal for attention, acceptance, tenderness, and the desire and need to overcome loneliness. The Worshipbook* of the United Presbyterian Church in the U. S. A. has a prayer (page 189) that reads in part: "We pray for prostitutes, who are victims of lovelessness, or of a craving to be loved. Keep us from easy blame and cruel dismissal." Lonely people who behave seductively may not want sex, they may be asking for friendship, a secure relationship. This is often the case when an adolescent has a "crush" on a teacher or youth minister. The consultant needs to avoid indulging his or her sexual needs by taking advantage of such persons.

b. Conversely, some people feel threatened by interpersonal closeness. They attempt to reduce interpersonal relationships to a single level of communication. This helps them avoid a more total, to them overwhelming, complex relationship. The seduction may actually be an attempt to generate distance by keeping the relationship one-dimensional.

Sexual exclusiveness is a way of saying, "If I know you only want one thing of me, I can handle that. If you want me to be 'many-splendored,' I am afraid I might not measure up to your expectations, so let's go to bed." Homosexuality may be one example of avoiding the multidimensional character of male-female relationship through narrowing one's world of people to a seemingly uncomplicated minority population.

c. Eroticism can be an expression of personalized hostility. Some prostitutes humiliate men in their profession. ("If he'll pay to sleep with me, he's nothing but a whoremongering fool.") The various degrees of the RAPO game described by the transactionalists have as a "payoff" the hurtful rejection of those who have been seduced, either before ("Don't you dare touch me! What gave you the idea I was *that* kind?") or after ("You'll pay for violating me!") a seduction is consummated.

Another way eroticism is an expression of hostility is the seemingly deliberate, although often "unconscious," practice of being attracted to one person (or sex) as a way of hurting another person or persons. The standard example of this is the marriage partner who is "frigid," "impotent," or "turned off" by his or her mate, yet has an affair flagrantly or demands a divorce, because of consuming attraction for "someone else." As analytic theory promises, such persons frequently then go through the same process with the paramour or the new spouse.

Many young homosexuals seek consultation because their choice of life-style causes great pain to their parents.

*Consultee:* I know how deeply I have hurt them! I talk with them and talk with them about my way of life, and it hurts them so! What would you suggest I do?

*Consultant:* [noting a broad smile on the face of the consultee throughout the above statement] Let me change the subject a moment before I attempt to answer your questions, OK?

*Consultee:* Anything you say. It grieves me so that I'm constantly hurting them so much!

*Consultant:* If you were ever to become angry with your parents and really wanted to hurt them badly, considering their value systems, attitudes, and so on, besides physical harm, how could you hurt them most?

*Consultee:* Why, become gay. They'll never understand my way of etc., and [grin, grin] they are in *such* pain, etc., etc.

The use of seductive behavior as a way of expressing hostility is a complex matter. Some congenitally attractive persons, the naturally beautiful, shapely, rich-voiced, handsomely featured seem incapable of being other than apparently seductive by virtue of their natural endowments. The sexually deprived are going to be "turned on" by them no matter what. Others, not so innately gifted, may have developed a capacity for compassion, empathy, and helpfulness which is seductive to the lonely, the frightened, the shy. No hostility is intended, but sooner or later the unintended seduction may evoke a response that leads to, "I'm sorry, but I think too much of you to take advantage of your needs. I'm flattered but, no." The rejection is painful, whether hostility is intended or not.

The wise consultant will know the risks involved in being nice to people, especially if the consultant is physically attractive. The thoughtful consultant should always be aware of the potential to hurt while in the very act of helping. Asking for or giving help of any kind is almost always seductive to some extent.

d. Eroticism can be an appeal for limits to be set when the erotically related person feels in danger of losing control. People sometimes fear they will lose moral control. They may resort to various devices to unattract others. These include unflattering attire, poor cosmetics, or personal hygiene, dieting to extreme, staying obese, acting crudely, etc. Other people who fear personal closeness will jeopardize their control, become overly forward, make coarse and grossly inappropriate advances in order to elicit rejection.

When one individual gives the appearance of losing control, others will exert control, set limits the individual feels incapable of setting upon himself or herself. Obvious examples of this are the objectionable behavior of drunks, overly tired children, and delinquent adolescents who manage to get strict limits imposed by external authorities, such as exasperated parents, the police, and juvenile authorities.

In short, some erotically related persons are asking others to prevent them from doing what they seem to want to do, but actually fear doing.

e. Erotic activity may be the attempt of some persons to establish a relationship at the highest level available to them at a given time. People on the verge of a "schizophrenic episode," feeling desperately isolated, lacking the usual interpersonal skills, at least temporarily, may throw themselves into frenzied sexual activity in order to retain the vestige of human contact.

f. Some people with limited capacity to separate symbols from realities may mistake sexual activity for love. The intellectually handicapped, as well as the "innocent" young, may confuse erotic behavior with the more complex, deeper subtleties of mature affection.

g. Still others may associate participation in sexual activity—or refraining from same—with independence. Adolescents may be striving for independence by acting out sexually—breaking with parental and "establishment" mores as a way of asserting their movement from dependency to independence. Impotent husbands and frigid wives may be declaring their lack of need for their spouses in the only way they can economically. For example, the father of four children cannot very well declare himself independent of need for his wife who stays home to care for the children so he can hold his job, but he can be independent of her at bedtime. Likewise the mother of four small children, who cannot economically manage without her husband's paycheck, can prove she does not need him in a romantic sense. Hostility may figure prominently in all such rebellions, as do other disguised emotions. The most common of these are emotions arising from the "unresolved oedipus complex," the discovery of which has brought Freud so much appreciation and condemnation.

h. Character suicide, reputation suicide, professional suicide, may be committed through sexual acting out as has been mentioned in another section of this book.

i. The search for identity involves many dimensions of human endeavor. One of these is the sexual. As Erikson has made obvious, adolescent sexual behavior is not essentially a rebellion, a failure of discipline, or the loss of morality. It is the experimental attempt, through handling one's body, to find out "Who am I?"—to establish identity.

The pathological parallel to such adolescent experimentation to determine identity is found in mental hospitals among supposedly "abnormal" persons who are trying to prove that in at least one way they are "normal."

j. Essentially, the erotically related person's behavior is interpreted by the competent consultant as a *cry for help.*

1) Do not initially condemn the erotically related person—consider all aspects of their situation, not just the moral.

2) Do not ignore the moral and social aspects affecting the erotically related person, because these are a part of the reality we represent as effective consultants.

3) Be frank, honest, accepting, but maintain sufficient professional structure so your warmth does not mislead or confuse the consultee more than is inevitable. (I. e., no sharing of how your spouse does not understand you either, no consultations in parked automobiles in isolated areas, etc. Stay in the barnyard, not the hayloft, in the supermarket aisle, not the cocktail lounge, etc.)

4) Recognize your own feelings and needs and discuss these with another professional person (not your spouse) who is competent to handle such emotionally laden consulting.

5) Assist the person in discovering the underlying cause of her or his preoccupations with sex. The experienced consultant can usually determine most of these in the first fifteen minutes of conversation on the subject. Time, the establishment of the fact that you take them seriously as persons, and patient "leading to insight" will accomplish the consultee's realization of what they seek, what they are doing. When we know what we are doing (intellectually *and emotionally*) we can be masters rather than slaves of our temptations and behavior.

6) Recognize and accept your limitations. Few of us can work helpfully with every person or every kind of person.

Dr. Wayne Oates has said, "The erotically related person comes to us as an attractively wrapped package. Our task is to examine the package just enough and no more, to get the package to the rightful recipient."

St. Paul has written that "No temptation has overtaken you that is not common to man," and that nothing "will be able to separate us from the love of God in Christ Jesus." Not even sex.

## 27. Suspicion

Because of past hurts, the suspicious person distrusts everyone. This may vary in intensity from the mildly wary individual who seems always complaining about how "out to get you" everyone is, to the dangerously deluded individual who believes plots are afoot. Such people are often intelligent, capable, and quite successful financially. They view all of life as a power structure and individual relationships as power struggles. They cannot abide any hint of weakness and go to sometimes extraordinary lengths to demonstrate their own strength. They usually lack true personal warmth, although may, when you initially meet them, exude an oily cordiality. Such persons often are devious and work out plots of their own which they feel are justified in their view of life.

They seem incapable of insight into their own personality dynamics. They talk convincingly, logically, and often get others to represent their causes, make accusations for them, and pit individuals and groups against one another. They lack a sense of sympathy or empathy with the needs and feelings of others, but possess an "exquisite sensitivity in interpersonal relations" to the point that they often are offended by the most minor events. For example, one woman helped considerably with her neighbor's daughter's wedding. Then she received an invitation in which the reception card was inadvertently left out by one of the bridesmaids who helped with the posting. She saw this as a desire to exclude her from the celebration "after all I've done for that girl." She refused to attend the wedding despite many attempts at reassurance and told others how she had been "stabbed in the back by people I'd always thought were my best friends."

Such people often have grandiose ideas of their own importance. They do not recognize any human shortcoming in themselves. When they are threatened by an impulse or thought that is to them unacceptable, they "project" the blame onto others, concealing from themselves their own part in the "unacceptable." This projective mechanism can run from the most mundane (*"They* gave me a C this semester") to the highly dangerous delusions and hallucinations experienced by assassins who are convinced they are right in following the instructions of the voices they hear in killing public officials.

There are a few simple rules that should enable one to consult with the inordinately suspicious person effectively:

The first is to realize that these people want and need emotional distance. They do not like to be crowded or backed into a corner. Providing the emotional distance they need may seem cool-hearted if not downright hard-hearted to those of us reared in the "love one another" atmosphere of American religions. Not doing *anything* for them that they might be able to do for themselves is one way of providing distance. Making sure you know what the person asks before offering anything is another. Respecting the mode of communication the suspicious person chooses is another. For example, if the person writes a "crank" letter, respond by letter, not by telephone or personal visit. If the person gossips about you and you learn of this, ask your informant to carry a message back, rather than ignoring the gossip (which would cause the suspicious person to believe the gossip more firmly) or rushing personally to confront or placate (which would threaten the person, or cause them to think you a weakling).

*good advice*

Be calm, firm, cool in relating to the person. Do not get involved in her or his emotional embroilments. If you must say something positive or complimentary, "wrap the gift in barbwire." Too much direct praise increases the suspicion in such people. Do not say, "You look lovely this evening" or "That was a wonderful job you did with the church festival." Say, "I'm sure you're not interested in my opinion, but you look all dressed up tonight," or "You probably got everyone else to do all the work, but you or somebody did a fine job with the church festival you were supposed to be chairperson for." A mildly grumpy attitude will relax the suspicious person in your presence.

Never do anything deceitful in relation to suspicious people. What you have to say about them, say *to* them, not about them behind their backs. For example, do not exclude them from a function because they are troublemakers, and then tell them it's because they are of the wrong age group. Just tell them, "Mr. Smith, I've asked that you not be on the Supper Committee because, as many talents as you have, I think your presence would impede the progress of the committee. You like to fuss so much, you'd serve better on the Social Action Committee." Such firmness can be offered with a sense of humor but your meaning should be clear and direct.

Suspicious people are often lonely, not well-liked, and an embarrassment to their families. They should *not* be avoided. Respectful, matter-of-fact attention means a lot to them. Tactful honesty is a must. ("You have a right to your opinion, which I feel is in error.")

Suspicious people will respect strength when they sense it. They can be productive colleagues if we don't get too close. They can almost always resolve their difficulties. Our assurance to them of this, or at least our observation that, "You have done everything you can in this circumstance. I have no suggestions for you. Let me know how it goes," will often assist them to feel affirmed, even in defeat.

With the suspicious person, respecting privacy and the need for distance —and "letting live"—is the avenue to effective consultation. Should such a person become increasingly agitated and possibly dangerous, medical and legal counsel is imperative, if not for the consultee, at least for the consultant.

Sections 28 and 34 contain some further comments regarding danger and crisis.

Suspicious people tend to appear incredibly naive. Repeatedly they will "trust" others, having unrealistically high expectations of them. They are then always being "let down," "done in," "stabbed in the back," etc. They set themselves up to be let down time after time.

A direct, firm confronting of them with their naiveté is repeatedly necessary to assist them in recognizing their unrealistic pseudo-trust. This can be done with humor. ("You've got to be more paranoid when you first meet people.") A cool accepting, not a cold rejecting attitude, is necessary, always.

## 28. Despair

Persons in despair have the facial appearance of despondency. They speak in subdued tones and express a sense of futility about life generally and of worthlessness about themselves specifically. They often have sleep disturbances—many awaken unrefreshed very early in the morning and are unable to go back to sleep. Others tend to sleep "all the time." They seem to brood and may feel great guilt, often over rather minor "sins" in the distant past. They may weep frequently, with little provocation. They also have eating troubles—most have no appetite and lose weight, although some may overeat and become obese. They seem to have lost interest in socializing, working, sexual activities, and experience a severe fading of religious faith.

Such persons may have the idea that they have some terminal illness and may seriously contemplate suicide. Many will speak openly about their intention to die, some may keep that a secret. Contrary to popular misconception, people who talk about suicide *do* attempt to take their own lives in a large percentage of cases. So such talk, whether direct ("I've thought of just ending it all") or indirect ("I know that if I can drive on across the bridge each morning and get to work, I'll make it through the day"), should be taken seriously.

Another characteristic of the despairing person is indecision over many matters, even trivial ones. ("I haven't been to church lately because I can't decide which shoes to wear.") Indecision over minor matters reflects indecision over major matters, such as whether to live or die.

Headache, backache, gastrointestinal distress, and other physical symptoms may accompany despair. Sudden uncharacteristic, unwise actions such as heavy drinking by a normally sober person, sexual misbehavior, financially ruinous ventures, may all be expressions of the despairing person's attempts at "character suicide." Politicians and clergy seem especially prone to misuse

76

of public funds or sexually unacceptable behavior when in despair. Physicians abuse drug laws, and bankers are fiscally irresponsible, while teachers tend toward illicit conduct with students as ways of committing "professional suicide."

There are three major areas of causal factors in despair. One is medical. There are a variety of medical causes that range from inadequate diet, body infections or parasites, to circulatory disorders and brain tumors.

A second major area is the social, and usually involves an experience of significant loss. This may be the loss of self-esteem among the victims of prejudice, the loss of status, prestige, money, position, "strength of youth," being needed, ability to function or to feel "fully human" in the case of the aging, the paraplegic or quadriplegic, those with spinal injury, mastectomy, sight or hearing loss, etc. Most frequently encountered by the pastoral consultant is the loss of significant other persons through death, divorce, or desertion. Traditional role loss is experienced by mothers whose nests empty as the children leave home and by mandatory retirement "victims" whose whole life was wrapped up in their work. Crusaders who finally win the Cause and feel no longer useful, whose life-purpose seems to end when their goals are realized, may, like Alexander the Great when he crossed the Indus, weep because there are no more worlds to conquer. Likewise, hard workers whose dreams never become actuality may suffer the despair of defeat and failure, just as the victors may suffer the despair of triumph.

A third cause of despair may be internalized anger—anger turned against the self rather than toward those with whom one is angry. The ultimate expression of externalized anger is homicide. The ultimate expression of internalized anger is suicide. Those of us trained in the Christian virtues of never letting the sun go down on our wrath are especially prone to this latter kind of despair.

If the despair has a medical cause, spiritual ministry will seldom cure the cancer. If loss is the cause, not assisting the person to grieve appropriately can lead to mental illness. If internalized anger is the causal factor, all the assurance of pious heaven that God forgives old sins will miss the mark, make the person go more deeply into despair, because anger, not guilt, is the real problem.

The effective consultation of the despairing person, therefore, includes:

1. Accurate diagnosis with appropriate referrals and consultation based on the consultee's needs.

2. Frequent brief visits in person, by telephone and letter. Five minutes a day, five days a week does more good than an hour once a week when internalized anger is the problem.

3. Getting the person to let you do something for him or her. This is *not* the time to be "client-centered" or "non-directive" or Adult-Adult. This is not the time for the despairing person to make decisions about shoes or suicide. "Let me make the decisions for you! You must promise me that you will not do *anything* significant, from business deals to quitting school to killing yourself without first talking this over with me or with someone whose opinions you respect!"

Or, "You *have* to go to the doctor. I'll dial the office for you to make the appointment right now and I'll drive you over there!"

Or, "I know you want to believe that your child is in heaven singing with the angels, but you need someone to listen how you first learned of the death. Tell me about it now!"

4. Getting the person to do something for someone else. "I can see that you are barely able to talk, but I need a cup of coffee. Let's go to the kitchen and you put some water on to boil." Or, "You can ease my burden in all this if you will agree to see the doctor right away. Will you do that for me, even though you don't feel you're worth wasting the doctor's time?"

5. Only under supervision should a consultant attempt to assist the person in gradually uncovering hidden internalized anger. The anger, once triggered into full awareness, can be highly explosive. The consultant who undertakes such a task should have all insurance policies in force lest the anger be unleashed on the consultant. Clinical training in teamwork consultation is essential for this kind of work.

6. Providing a future for the person in despair will assist them as they move from despair to hope. This is often quite simply done by promising to telephone the person at a certain time and getting their assurance that they will be alive to answer the telephone (doing something for them). Or, asking that the person telephone the consultant at a certain time, then being sure to be available (getting the person to do something for you). At the time of the telephone call, another "appointment" is set, providing another segment of future. "I'll be at the store at ten in the morning. See you then."

Above all, letting people in despair know that you care and are "with them" as representatives of "Emmanuel—God with us" will help.


## 29. Confusion

Before the Tower of Babel and after the Day of Pentecost, instances of confusion are reported or implied in Scripture.

Adam and Eve were no doubt confused when expelled from Eden. The Israelites, wandering in the wilderness for forty years, or during the days of the Judges when "every man did what was right in his own eyes," must have experienced bewilderment. The Old Testament is in part a history of conflict between true and false prophecy, wise and foolish leadership, and the only certainty often seemed uncertainty.

People who lived in New Testament times were also exposed to confusing events and ideas. Political and economic as well as traditional religious attitudes and beliefs were challenged by Christ. When the promised kingdom was at hand, Christ was crucified, not crowned. The bulk of the books of the New Testament are attempts to interpret the chaos of first-century life in some orderly way, to clarify confusion.

If anything, people get more confused more often in our modern world than they did in Biblical times.

Confusion is the experience of being bewildered, disturbed, uncomprehending, uncertain, and at a loss as to what to think, say, or do.

Being confused can run from the relatively mild experience of not being certain how one should plan her or his day in order to "get it all done," to the almost panicky sense of being out of contact with reality with which workers and patients in mental hospitals are familiar.

Confusion has many causes. Confusion can be caused by the routine difficulties of everyday life—"I am confused as to what to do about our teenage daughter. She wants to go to a party that will not end until the wee hours of the morning"—to the confusion that arises from extraordinary and cataclysmic events, such as an earthquake, a tornado, an automobile wreck, a hotel fire, a war, etc.

Confusion may be caused by a physical disorder such as a high fever, a serious infection, being exhausted, or undernourished. It may be caused by the shortage of oxygen to the brain which sometimes afflicts us as we get older. People who indulge in alcohol or take drugs to excess may be confused.

Unusual experiences such as being lost in a forest or in a desert or in the darkness or even in a large unfamiliar building may confuse us. Presumably, the people in the astronaut program would become quite confused if one of their space ships were to get lost in space. The confusion of stage fright, mike fright, blocking on a test, starting a new job, or getting married is an experience which many of us have had.

When we experience excessive emotion, we may feel confused. When we lose a loved one through death or when we are ignored or hurt by significant other people, we may experience confusion. Trouble at work, being demoted or fired from a job may cause us to be confused. Any time we have strong ambivalence, feel pulled in two directions, we experience confusion. The "double-minded man" of Scripture was "unstable in all his ways." The apostle Paul wrote, "I am pulled in two directions." (Phil. 1:23, TEV)

Sometimes very positive experiences can lead to confusion. For example, winning a prize in a contest might cause us to be uncertain as to what to do or how to react. A girl may be confused and uncertain when a young man proposes to her, being overwhelmed with unexpected positive feelings.

Some confusional states are progressive and irreversible. Others are transient and respond to "treatment." *Everyone* can be helped to some extent.

When a person seems to be confused in a serious way, a medical specialist or a psychologist should make a diagnosis and prognosis. A clergyperson or a Christian layperson without special training is not ordinarily qualified for this specific work.

However, we may encounter someone who seems to be confused, bewildered, or in a daze, and want to try to be helpful to the person until more competent assistance can be secured.

1. First, it is helpful to try to establish the boundaries of identity. We do this by telling the person who we are and what we are. Even if the person is acquainted with us, when confused he or she may momentarily forget. It is not a good idea to ask such questions as, "You *do* remember me don't you?" It is better to speak in simple declarative sentences, even risking insulting the other person's intelligence. For example, one might say to a confused person something like, "My name is John Smith. I am a neighbor. I live across the street. Would you tell me your name?" or, "Can you tell where you are wanting to go?"

2. Another way to help is to ask questions such as: "Have you been hurt?" or, "Have you taken some kind of medicine recently?" We might also ask the person, "Have you had something to drink?" or, "Have you been drinking heavily and quit?" Another question that we might raise is, "Have you ever had fainting spells or seizures of any kind?"

If the person answers yes to any of these questions or if you feel that the answer to these questions might be yes, you may well have a medical emergency on hand. It is a good idea to get the person in touch with their family physician or a doctor whom you know. In some communities it is a good idea to take the person to the emergency room at a local hospital. Christian faith and concern is no substitute for medical attention if medical attention is needed. Getting a person to proper professional attention is an expression of Christian faith and effective consultation.

3. Another question which we might raise with a seemingly confused person is, "Have you been like this before?" If the person says or indicates the answer is yes, then we might ask the person, "What was helpful to you last time?" Even very confused persons may remember what is helpful to them.

4. With a bewildered person we may need to set limitations which they are unable to set for themselves. For example, if a person seems uncertain where

they are going or what they want to do, we may say something to them such as, "Please sit down here on the steps so that we can talk. Perhaps that would be helpful."

5. We might need to adapt ourselves to the level of limitations possible to the other person. If the confused person seems so agitated as to be unable to sit down, walking side by side and talking may be preferable to trying to make him or her sit down to talk. In such an instance as this, we first adjust to the agitated person's pace, then gradually slow her or him down by example.

6. Always try to speak in short simple direct sentences. Avoid saying or asking more than one thing at a time.

7. Sometimes when people are mildly confused, assigning a simple familiar task may help. For example, if a woman has just received news of the loss of a loved one, she may not be sure what to say or do. A simple request such as, "Could you make a cup of instant coffee for us?" might give the uncertain person some familiar, "automatic" routine to do until they "get hold of themselves."

8. Simple assurance gently suggested is preferable to over-assurance especially of the demanding type. It is good to say something like, "You seem somewhat uncertain but you will be safe if you will stay here. You may become less confused in a little while." It is not so helpful to anxiously shout demands for assurance such as, "You understand don't you? Sure you do! Why yes, say you do!"

9. Simplifying the environment of the confused person can be helpful.

When elderly people go out for a walk, it is more assuring to them, even if a bit boring to their companion, if they follow the same familiar route each day, going in and out of the same exits and entrances. People who tend to be chronically confused, such as certain elderly people, do not adjust comfortably to spontaneous schedules. It is much better for them to follow routine and to have a good habit system. Elderly people, for example, often do not sleep well in any bed other than their own. This can interfere with family plans for vacations and holidays. However, if we bear in mind their need for a simplified and habitual routine, we will realize that they are not just being stubborn and cranky. They are attempting to function at their best.

Many elderly people are much more comfortable with a light on in their bedroom at night so that if they awaken they can orient themselves quickly. Getting up in a dark room, even a familiar dark room, can add confusion.

In addition to routine, repetition may be necessary with confused people. A nursing home chaplain quickly learns that certain residents enjoy visits but forget who the chaplain is from one visit to the next. Re-introducing oneself to a confused person may avoid further confusion.

10. Recognizing and taking seriously the personhood of other people is essential in assisting them if they are confused. We should never treat another person as if he or she were less than human, no matter how disoriented they may seem to us. We should always act as if the person might understand, even if this seldom happens. "People can only be as responsible as we let them."

One of the best ways to help ourselves when we confront confusion in our own lives is to attempt to plan ahead for that which may be confusing. This includes the routine safety precautions that we all so often take for granted but which can be so important. Remembering or reminding ourselves as to the location of exits and fire extinguishers, posting the telephone number of the police and fire departments prominently near the telphone, thinking about, talking about, and planning for possible emergencies in the home, on a trip, etc., may well provide us with the resources we need when confusion comes.

It is also good to prepare a list of people in whom we have confidence and to whom we can turn in times of confusion. Trusted people, professional helpers as well as personal friends, may often be the greatest antidote to confusion when it strikes. For example, a relatively simple matter like a subtraction mistake in one's checkbook may cause us bewilderment when the bank notifies us that we are overdrawn. We may for a few moments not know what to do and feel something of panic. A telephone call to one's banker resolves such problems quickly with a minimum of confusion. We may not think about doing such a simple thing when the actual event takes place, unless we have planned ahead and in some fashion left a reminder such as the name and telephone number of the banker in our checkbook. Such precautions help us avoid moments, hours, or even whole nights of anxiety and confusion. The same kind of thing may hold true in working with our families, children, and fellow employees. If we can plan ahead what we ought to do when something goes wrong or crisis comes, half of the battle may be over.

In the final analysis, we ought to have some trusted friends including members of our family who will know what we would like to have done for us and with us should confusion come to us. One of the least confusing experiences in my life was the arrangement for my own mother's funeral. Having been very close to my mother for many years, I expected that when she passed away I would be plunged into considerable confusion as well as grief and anxiety. However, she left instructions as to exactly how she would like her funeral conducted, who the minister would be, what clothing she wanted to be "layed out" in, and which cemetery she preferred. These instructions enabled me not only to avoid confusion in a very painful crisis time in my own life, but also enabled me to be sure that her own wishes were carried out.

In a similar fashion, I think we can tell family or friends what we would like done for us should we have emotional problems, medical problems, or other stressful situations which would eventuate in our being too confused to think clearly and plan carefully for ourselves.

Ultimately, the Christian confronts confusion armed with certain assurances which enable us to survive. It is no mistake or accident that the very elderly seem to become very religious. When confidence in this life and this world fades and the end seems near, a return to the eternal promises of our gospel and our Savior can enable us to survive even the most complex crisis with dignity, hope, and peace. The one thing that the Christian can always remember is that no matter how confused we may be, our God is always in command, in love for us all. "Who shall separate us from the love of Christ? Shall tribulation, or distress, or persecution, or famine, or nakedness, or peril, or sword? . . . No, in all these things we are more than conquerors through him who loved us. For I am sure that neither death, nor life, nor angels, nor principalities, nor things present, nor things to come, nor powers, nor height, nor depth, nor anything else in all creation, will be able to separate us from the love of God in Christ Jesus our Lord." (Romans 8:35, 37–39)

## 30. Dependency

One goal of human life, indeed of all existence in our universe is, ideally, mutually supportive *interdependence*. The idea that anyone or anything can or should be truly independent is a fiction useful only to human beings at certain brief episodes in the pilgrimage of life, if at all. Even the strongest in society or in the jungle depend on someone or something in a mutually supportive way.

Mutual interdependence cannot be static. As the young grow, so must the parents. There is a time when parents must feed their young and assist them in elimination, as well as sleep with them. The time comes when the young must learn to feed on their own, be "trained," and sleep alone, or pathology will result.

There is no such thing as perfect mutual interdependence since conflicts are inevitable when people are really people.

This section is intended to outline the types and situations involved in *excessive dependency*.

1. Excessive dependency of the *transient type* is normal in emotionally healthy people during times of stress. The recently bereaved, the sick or injured, the "temporarily financially embarrassed," the person between jobs, and even the non-alcoholic who has had "a little too much" may be in need of the care one provides for the transiently excessively dependent. Support, appropriate infor-

mation at appropriate times, the right help given in the right way at the right time are basic skills essential for the effective consultant. Assisting someone to locate a reputable funeral director, physician, visiting nurse, financial adviser and bank loan officer, reliable employment agency, driving an inebriated friend home from a party, or even recommending the best cure for a hangover (if there is such a thing) may all be examples of appropriate assistance to the transiently excessive dependent person. When the immediate need ends, the help should end. Consultants who persist in pushing the grief process after acute mourning ends, or worrying people that they might lose another job or about finances or swamping the occasional drinker with statistics about the evils of Demon Rum may indicate an unhelpful need of the consultant to be depended on.

2. Excessive dependency among those severely *deprived* during the "formative years" and over considerable spans of time is quite different from transient dependency. Seriously deprived persons do not need just brief support. They need support and support systems throughout life. At the risk of sounding completely deterministic psychologically, I believe that some people have suffered from the lack of emotional and other kinds of nurture during early life (childhood, early adolescence) that has a permanent effect on them. Such people, whether the victims of uncaring parents, separation from parent figures by illness, war, natural disaster, or whatever, seem to have an excessive need to depend on others that is never fully met.

One psychologist, not derisively for she is a true lover of animals, described such individuals as "dog-like people who follow you around, seem to lick your hand, and never get enough patting."

The great danger in relating to such persons is that the consultant is touched deeply by their needs, wants to nurture and protect, then feels "hounded" by them, and eventually lashes out angrily. This adds one more rejection and hurt to people who have been rejected and hurt for a lifetime.

The manner of being helpful to such folk is to structure the time and attention given them. Several brief conversations at regular times each week, plus very short telephone calls at prescribed intervals will provide the deprived person regular nurture without overloading the consultant's schedule or emotional reserve.

A sharply clear contract is essential in such situations. "Our agreement is that we meet for coffee on Wednesday afternoons and you are to telephone me on Monday evening for five minutes during the halftime of the football game. I will also be seeing you, but we cannot talk for long, after church services."

The encouragement of support systems including church, civic, social, and other activities from which deprived people may derive recognition and appreciation is very important. With such persons the development of all kinds of opportunities for affirmation is effective consultation.

Every experienced pastor knows who the deprived are in the flock and knows they can always be counted on to help swell the crowd at church suppers or fill the carload needed to insure the success of Billy Graham's Youth Crusade at the ball park. Since many emotionally deprived excessively dependent people have talents and skills, not to mention financial resources and eagerness to serve, they are an important segment of the parish and should never be ignored for practical as well as pious purposes.

3. _Constitutionally_ dependent persons include the mentally retarded and the physically handicapped. Effective consultation with them is based on the most important non-canonical commandment of all—"Thou shalt not do anything for anyone that he or she can do for himself or herself!" About 20% of the population have some physical or mental handicap. They are seldom seen in worship services in such high percentage. Constructing buildings and grounds for the physically handicapped, with ramps and rails, developing a free "taxi service" within the parish, and assisting the mentally retarded to develop good habit systems will not only help them to help themselves, but will usually swell any worship service attendance and most annual budgets of churches.

Some mentally handicapped individuals may need special protection—for example retarded young girls or boys who lack the intellectual ability to determine whom to trust when they need guidance and rules, much as young children are protected from accepting rides or candy from strangers.

The consultant who takes everyone seriously as a person, refrains from unrealistic ambitions for those who cannot realize the unrealizable, and who firmly, yet with love, rejects the inner need to overindulge the handicapped, will do well.

Sometimes a clinical experience is worth a dozen books in assisting the consultant to accurately perceive the true needs of the constitutionally dependent. You do not need to enroll in an expensive course for this. Just borrow a wheelchair and get around in it for an afternoon, or, with a friend's help, spend the morning wearing a blindfold. My own experience with a severe case of laryngitis taught me more about working helpfully with the mute and deaf than a whole summer of clinical training.

4. _Severe_ dependency. "Symbiosis" means "life-together." A symbiotic team is one in which each person in the team relinquishes certain self-functions which the other partner assumes. The classic example usually given is the mother who gives enemas to her child several times a day in order for the child to eliminate. Without the mother the child may not be able to eliminate and internal

poisoning can ensue. The mother, of course, can thus never be gone from the child for very long and her world of work, and socialization, becomes inextricably bound up with the child. In time, other self-functions are exchanged and the bonds of parent-child love become chains. When the child is asked a question, the mother answers. The mother cannot sleep without the child in bed beside her. This is not unusual with a two- or three-year-old child. The average college or military base frowns on such relationships when the child is twenty.

Repressed and/or expressed hostility mounts in direct proportion to the degree of dependency. Hostile wishes that are "unconscious" become fears for the safety or well-being of the symbiotic partner. "Separation anxiety," not uncommon when toddlers enter day-care facilities, becomes unhealthy when teenagers wish to attend a ball game or dance at the high school, and assumes sinister proportions when thirty-five-year-olds are unable to leave home to look for a job.

One mother, whose six-year-old screamed when left at the door of the first-grade classroom, was encouraged by the teacher to have the child evaluated by a pediatrician. After careful history-taking and physical examination, the doctor handed the mother a prescription.

"When do I give her the pills?" she asked.

"You don't. You take the pills while she screams," she answered. The doctor's orders were followed and no "symbiotic childhood schizophrenic disorder" developed.

Most young people need to get away from home by degrees, if they are to develop the capacity for mutual interdependence. When parents are "too strict" in disallowing gradual emancipation, children may run away. The hippie communes and drug culture groups of the 1960s were populated by a number of adolescents from very good homes, very protective homes, who, like the prodigal son, felt they had to break away lest they never be able to leave.

When the consultant is confronted by a symbiotic partnership, the risk is very high that any intervention may cause serious results. Often, when one symbiotic partner breaks away, the other breaks down. When the elderly mother finally passes on, the dutiful daughter who had always stayed with her may seek another maternal symbiotic partner such as the state mental hospital. When the spouse of an alcoholic finally grows weary of feeding, changing, rescuing the alcoholic—and perhaps the accompanying beatings—and secures a divorce, the next marriage may well be to another alcoholic. One does not wonder how the prodigal son "made out." No doubt he made it. But what did the elder brother do when the parent passed on?

Where symbiosis is concerned the ethical consultant will resist trying to play God by forcing choices between unhealthy dependent relatedness and psychotic episodes.

In summary, in other terms, there are four types of dependency:

86

1. Passive dependency—as seen in children and emotionally healthy persons under stress who *need* to depend on the consultant and other supporting persons temporarily, and deprived and constitutionally dependent persons who need *structured* and *regulated* long-term support, but not indulgence.

2. Dominant-dependent persons who wish to depend upon others such as dependent parents who need to depend on others to take risks, but want to "call the shots," or the "alcoholic" spouse, who really cannot provide for or care for the household but is a despotic tyrant whose rule is law and who is "never wrong."

3. Double-minded dependency which is normal in adolescents who depend on parents but defy the parental rules and regulations. The stereotype of this is the "independent" hippie types who carry the parents' credit cards to support their self-declared freedom.

4. Pathological dependency which is technically catalogued as "symbiotic schizophrenia."

Effective consultation in each situation is summarized as follows:

A. In transient dependency situations provide what is needed appropriately at the appropriate time and no more. Structure and contract are the clues to effective consultation with the constitutionally and deprived dependent persons.

B. Assistance in the "weaning process" for the victims of dominant dependence, and support for the "forsaken parent" or the deserted alcoholic are effective consultation procedures.

C. With the double-minded dependent person, time, life, and the conscious or unconscious motives of both the dependent and the dependee are crucial. Adolescents grow up. "Life is the only therapist who never asks, 'Can the patient tolerate the treatment?' " The double-minded dependent cannot survive after the credit cards are canceled unless they "mature" and become responsible. Before that happens, the consultant can only "stand and wait" and be available for whatever Dumping she or he can tolerate.

D. Psychiatric consultation and being prepared for drastic results from intervention in symbiosis are necessary when the consultant is asked to assist in breaking up such severe pathology.

A final note is in order on the tendency toward dependency in the consultant. Those who are fortunate enough to have been "fed" psychologically and spiritually, appropriately at each stage of their development will be able to consult effectively and not be damaged when their consultative efforts are rejected.

Those who have lacked essential psychological and spiritual nurture in their life pilgrimage will either refuse to be mutually interdependent, i. e. not have consultants of their own, or be so dependent on their consultees that no one can depend on them.

Consultants still dependent on their own parent figures cannot effectively consult with others. They cannot take the risks essential in the precarious, inexact science/art of consulting. They are either "pure Parent" or so "non-directive" as to be of no help.

Some consultants may have been so overfed emotionally and spiritually that they may lack empathy, never comprehend what others are up against. Clinical training under qualified supervision may cure this—sometimes a butcher knife or hatchet helps more than waiting for scalpel and anesthesia when battlefield conditions exist.

## 31. Manipulation

Every intact person knows that he or she is manipulative in relationships. All of us consciously or unconsciously have little interpersonal devices, learned no doubt from parent figures, childhood acquaintances, admired authorities, professional performers, etc., which we use to extract from others what we want. In times of stress we may resort to such devices out of necessity for "survival." The situation may be financial embarrassment when we put our "best foot forward" to favorably impress a bank loan officer.

Some people must become expert at manipulation in order to earn a living in a specific profession such as selling, interrogating suspects, raising funds, or saving souls.

Adroitness in explaining how we came into the possession of someone else's pencil in second-grade homeroom, socks and sweatshirts from the college athletic department, or why a different shade of lipstick or a different brand of cigarette stubs have appeared on our shirts or in our ashtrays has become a nervously accepted part of the American Way of Life.

There are those, however, for whom manipulation is the basic mode of relating to others. Such people have two questions whenever they encounter any other person. Question #1 is, "What does she or he have that I want?" Question #2 is, "What do I need to do to get it?" Cheap, tawdry county-seat carnivals and plush Wall Street brokerage houses, as well as Hollywood and the revival circuit, are populated by such persons.

Extractive-manipulative persons are those who "love things and use people." They fall into three categories.

The first are the successful manipulators who never get caught. They make rather excellent statespersons, presidents, and dictators, Academy Award-winning artists, leading pulpiteers, financiers, professional athletes, gamblers, and criminals. They are usually in the higher income brackets (non-taxable or unreported, of course).

The rules by which they live and operate are usually few and simple: "Never give a sucker an even break." "Professional gamblers don't" (gamble, that is—the fix is always in or they won't play). "Know what the other person wants and provide it convincingly," etc. Some people yield to intimidation by Enforcers, others are rendered vulnerable by clumsy, pathetic, sob-story behavior. The successful manipulator is adept at being anything and anyone you want him or her to be in order for you to give up your savings, your vote, your virginity, your cash, or whatever.

A second category includes the small-time hustlers, chiselers, backroad evangelists, used-car salespersons, pornographic distributors, racetrack tipsters, card or pool sharks, small-time golf pros, limited-success politicians, gurus of occult religion-sciences, and writers of second-rate books on counseling. They seldom get caught at anything, but they never make a million dollars either.

The third category includes the inadequate manipulators who populate the prison systems of the world, die of acute alcoholic or other overdose poisoning, or suffer other social and biological terminal diseases.

A convenient system for categorizing these three levels of chronically manipulative persons is to think of them in terms of certain sexual offenders in American society. There are high-priced call girls (who usually graduate with the passage of time into the cosmetic empire); the prostitutes (who end up tending bar in order to support legal or "common law" husbands); and the whores who die from brutal assault in or out of prisons.

High-priced "call girls" in the religious world may be invited to pray at national political conventions, visit the White House, and live (luxuriously) on non-taxable "love gifts."

The religious parallel to the prostitute operates a barely legal private practice in pastoral counseling without benefit of any national certification or accreditation.

The whores "lift" an offering at tent meetings or in storefront churches in order to support their heavy drinking. They often have their throats slit for a $55.61 offering in the alley behind the storefront or get shotgunned by moonshiners on lonely country roads for a similar amount.

The extractive-manipulative person can only operate successfully so long as the rest of society are interested in getting something of worth for nothing or nearly nothing. Games of chance, from the county fair midway to Vegas or Monaco, would be out of business tonight if most of us did not have a touch of the extractive within us.

The consultant *must* be in touch with her or his own extractive-manipula-

89

tive tendencies in order to even recognize this disorder in others. Greenwald's classic monograph "Treatment of the Psychopath" describes this essential in entertaining detail.

The hallmarks of manipulative behavior are easily recognizable:

1. First, these people *do* what the rest of us *fantasize.* They actually take people's money, virtue, loyalty, or whatever it is that *you* would secretly like to get from people. Everybody enjoys reading about a successful "con," whether in fact or fiction. The exploits of adventurers, seducers, brilliant detectives, 99%-successful psychotherapists, and "white god" missionaries thrill most people. Lurid accounts of gangland slayings, vicious rapes, incinerated automobile race car drivers, even *The Rise and Fall of the Third Reich* get vast readership if not Pulitzer Prizes. Who is not excited by the escape or the capture of a "don" of the Mafia?

Until we recognize and accept our own inclination toward the manipulative, we cannot recognize manipulators.

2. Manipulators are almost always highly articulate, convincing, winsome, verbally and/or athletically. Sullivan has termed such glibness as "sociopathic fluency."

3. Manipulators *imitate* what we would like to be at our best. When you meet someone who more than measures up to what you would be at your best, or how you might suffer under the worst of conditions, beware—you are about to be taken.

They have the ability to be "all things to all people." They are perfectly at home around the potbellied stove and cracker barrel and resplendent in dinner jackets. They have the ability to master any situation with grace, poise, dignity, or folksiness. Hence any "game" which requires convincing acting ability—from pulpit to stage to the political or sports arena—is their natural habitat.

4. There is a lack of deep or real feeling in their imitations. They may seem quite inhuman in their exploitations of others. They do not empathize. They delight in taking advantage of the disadvantaged as well as the advantaged. They rob rich and poor alike.

At times this inhumane quality reaches extremes in sadism. Cheating and lying, torturing and killing, considering those of no use to them as "nothings," they make excellent principals or underlings in organized crime, concentration camps, and guerrilla fighting, interrogators of suspects, managers of gambling, prostitution, or narcotics rings, as well as less malevolent con artistry. The epigraph to *The Godfather,* a quotation from Balzac, hints at the manipulative-extractive nature of the economic basis of the world—"Behind every great fortune there is a crime."

5. The manipulative person is _impulsive._ The demands of the moment must be satisfied _soon._ They do not work diligently for future rewards except in con games. They will botch a good thing as impulsively as they will enter a new intrigue. After several months of exquisitely painful planning and preparation to rip off a person or institution and get away with it, they may lose profits in a single impulsive indiscretion. "The criminal always returns to the scene of the crime" is not always true, but is based on professional police experience of the impulsive indiscretions of the extractive person.

6. The manipulator has a host of acquaintances, but no friends. She or he will weary every well-intentioned friend borrowing money, cashing rubber checks, seducing the friends' children, knowingly infecting them with venereal disease, wrecking or selling borrowed tools or automobiles, etc.

7. The manipulative person has a history of many jobs, and activities, as well as people with whom the manipulator has made an excellent first impression, shown exceeding promise, then "blown" the operation. Such persons drift from intrigue to intrigue, business to business, con to con, and person to person, never setting down roots of dependability and trustworthiness.

8. These people are usually described as being without feeling, although they evoke great feeling in their victims. At times, under conditions of great stress, when "the stakes are high," they may feel excitement. They hunt for danger and peril in order to experience "normal" human feelings. They thus make excellent spies, but if successful in avoiding suspicion, may become "double agents" to squeeze a little more excitement out of an already highly dangerous profession, not to mention increasing the monetary rewards.

In order to get clinical experience of how people react to the extractive-manipulative person, go through a few days doing nothing you are supposed to do, yet smiling a lot and complimenting and agreeing with those who question such practice. You'll get away with a lot. If you do not feel anxious during such an exercise, you will at least become more adept at the requirement under point 1 above.

A few paragraphs are in order regarding the dynamics which produce the extractive person. Theoretically, the manipulator has an "arrested ego development" during the first three years of life. It is normal for the infant who wants its bottle NOW to go through a progression of whimpering, crying, having a tantrum, until the bottle is provided. It is not "normal" for a twenty-two-year-old to go through such a progression of eliciting sympathy, exhibiting suffering, intimidating, and demanding immediate reward.

The manipulator has an "I'm OK—You're not OK" position, to use transactional terms. The works of Berne and Harris make this explicit. The status, money, position, sex, control, kicks, or whatever the manipulator desires are more important to him or her than the feelings, needs, or rights of others. Manipulators relate in Buber's "I-it" fashion.

Manipulators are the products of inconsistent parents who manipulate originally innocent children. They barter with the child for what the parents want, then cheat. "If you'll be real quiet all through church service, we'll get you an ice cream cone on the way home." The child is quiet. When the family car whizzes past the ice cream store, the child reminds the parents of their promise. The response is a harsh, or possibly oily, refusal to stop for some vague reason. The child ends up having been quiet and not getting ice cream. The child feels hurt.

In time the child made a decision not to feel any more hurt. The child learns to manipulate back. "No, I'll not be quiet in church for an ice cream con later. I'll be quiet for a dollar NOW!" The parents must then make a choice between a scene during the church service, or giving the dollar. Either way the child wins. If the scene takes place, a later beating reinforces the "I'm OK— You're not OK" position, adding fuel to the smoldering "sociopathy" in the young child.

The child must learn to extract attention, appreciation, and time, since nothing else seems to get such necessities for her or him. By age five or six the child practices deceptions and manipulations on unsuspecting playmates. Later, refined techniques work with school teachers, with the exception of the most experienced, who earn undeserved criticism from parents for their "harsh" attitudes. Social workers and police officers then become victims of the predatory adolescent's proficiency at promising "good" behavior in exchange for "one more chance." Judges next fall prey to the youthful manipulator's charms. ("I guess I sowed a few wild oats in my own youth and I've turned out all right.")

By late adolescence, the manipulator is on his or her way to success or tragedy, always leaving a wake of human heartbreak.

The successful consultant is REALLY up against *something* when confronted by a manipulative person. The manipulator only functions in a non-antisocial way when tightly bound by external controls. A former U. S. Navy officer once confided to me that he had absolutely the best crew on his ship that ever existed—"so long as we were at sea. When we hit port, within twelve hours every one of them was in jail or the brig depending on who got to them first, the Shore Patrol or the civilian police. They *had* to be between steel hulls to keep in line!"

Some manipulators realize this. They may deeply wish to be controlled. The classic example of this is the prison inmate who brilliantly escapes from a maximum-security unit, then robs a gasoline station at the edge of town and attempts to escape on a major highway *on foot.* He is immediately picked up by the local (hick) sheriff and returned for an extended sentence behind even tighter security, where he becomes again a "model prisoner" and sings baritone in the prison chapel choir.

Some successful work is currently being done with a few seasoned sociopaths (as the American Psychiatric Association's *Diagnostic and Statistic Manual of Mental Disorders* designates manipulators) by some treatment facilities. Usually the manipulator is assigned to a treatment team consisting of four to six therapists. The psychiatric nurse, social worker, clinical psychologist, psychiatrist, activity therapist, etc., work directly with the patient (their fees are paid in advance). They also meet regularly with another therapist who never meets the sociopath, never falls under the sway of her or his eloquence or seductiveness, and who assists them in unraveling the conflicts the patient has generated among them. (Manipulators early learn to pit authority figures against each other to the benefit of the manipulator. "Mommy said she loved me more than you, Daddy, because she gave me a quarter." "Here's a dollar. Now who loves you more?")

In any event, the consultant is up against nearly impossible odds when confronted by a truly manipulative-extractive artist. He or she must:

1. Be prepared to recognize manipulation when it happens. The best way to do this is to realize that "it takes one to know one."

2. Reject the manipulations as soon as detected. This should be done in calm "cold blood"—not "hot blood," since some manipulators derive their kicks from making "the grown-ups" angry. *Laughingly* pointing out the "con" to the manipulator indicates your expertise, hints that you know something about manipulation that she or he does not. *That* will "hook" the manipulator into respecting your competence. If you let them take you, they'll have no use for your counsel.

For example:

*Consultant:* Have you ever thought of becoming a Hollywood actress?
*Consultee:* Well, ah, [beaming] in a way, I guess. Why do you ask?
*Consultant:* The act you've been putting on for me—you're *almost* good!! With training, you could make it, maybe.
*Consultee:* [gulp! splutter-splutter] Whatever on earth do you mean? [verging on tears and/or anger]
*Consultant:* See what I mean—that was very close to being good.
*Consultee:* OK, wiseguy. What did I do wrong? [looking hard and intent, hoping to learn something]

3. Accept the talents of the person ethically *to enhance his or her self-esteem.* "You've got something going. Now let's see how you can get that something

going for You. You really are OK. You don't have to fake it anymore. If you stick with me, you'll see."

4. Assist in setting secure limits for the manipulator. This is difficult because there really is a sucker born every minute.

5. Rehabilitation begins with the person's recovery of how it feels to hurt. Rescuing her or him from the punishments of society will not accomplish this. Providing support during imprisonment or other punishment, *without* excusing or rationalizing his or her behavior, may indicate that everybody does not have a racket.

6. Never accept anyone's "story" without validation from other sources. This rules out counseling with individuals apart from consulting with family, social workers, police, etc.

7. If taken, drain your hostility to another professional—not against the manipulator directly. *Always* laugh with her or him—or *at least* be philosophical. Manipulators can teach you a lot. By venting wrath at them directly, you may cut off a valuable source of invaluable training.

8. Read Greenwald, Berne, and Cleckley. Regularly. Watch television—the cops-and-robbers shows, soap operas, political speeches, and above all the Evangelists.

9. Be armed with the knowledge that most sociopaths mellow or "burn out" between ages forty and sixty, or they get caught accepting bribes in Washington offices, depending on whether they are winners or losers. Or they are content to drink beer in their undershirts and watch "de fights" while being supported by martyr spouses or children. Or they convert their millions to philanthropic enterprises—endowing libraries or leukemia research or such.

10. Realize that your most effective consultation may be with the painfully deprived children of the manipulators. This may be done directly—"It is not a sin to recognize that your father [mother] is [was] no good. God bless you my child." Or indirectly through social activism.

As I write these words I am excruciatingly aware of this morning's newspaper sub-headlines. They describe the fate of a four-year-old girl. She was hospitalized for trauma caused by beatings inflicted by her parents when she was eleven months old. Because of some archaic laws, she was returned to her obviously sadistic parents who got their kicks from causing pain to others. Twice more she was admitted to the local general hospital suffering bruises and once a broken bone. At age four she was "admitted D.O.A." Police investigation disclosed that she had been required by her (drunken) parents to drink a bottle of Tabasco Sauce. When she resisted she was stripped nude and beaten as she ran screaming about the apartment until she finally submitted to drinking the painfully burning substance. She wept loudly following this, and to quiet her, the parents beat her to death.

"There oughtta be a law."

The consultant has an ethical responsibility to work for such a *law,* not out of rage, but out of compassion. When we cannot help the extractive-manipulator, we can help the victims.

This is effective consultation, if not in supermarket aisles or barnyards, then in legislative chambers.

One final note: There *may* be such a thing as manipulative persons who use their interpersonal skills, not for personal but humane purposes. They *may* use people for the general welfare of people. If so, the text is "be ye therefore wise as serpents, and harmless as doves." (Matt. 10:16, KJV) The effective consultant may follow this injunction of Christ, but only in "fear and trembling," continually checking out her or his inclinations with others whose judgment we respect, i. e. whose manipulations we not only admire, but also are convinced *are* for the welfare of people.

*part IV*
# Leavening
# the Bread

## Introduction to Part IV

Part I of this book helped you learn to find out what people want. Suggestions were given for your use in providing what people seek. Part II helps you comprehend hidden meanings in what people say and do, so that your pastoral practices will be relevant and appropriate. The third Part of this book is a resource to which you will wish to return for increasing practical comprehension of and working with different kinds of people.

In the final Part of this book you will receive practical information and guidelines for your use in consulting.

We will consider some ways which have been helpful in leading others to insight. We will also pay considerable attention to how you can improve your skills in working in emergency situations. Some typical emergency situations encountered by pastors will be presented in detail. A careful analysis of the successful handling of emergencies is also given.

There is a chapter discussing the ethical questions involved in the issue of professional and pastoral confidentiality. This gives you a workable and practical theory, which will help you in this sensitive area.

Another chapter is a statement of the way in which everyday pastoral practice can include evangelism most effectively. Another chapter describes the appropriate resource of prayer in your consultations. The way prayer can be managed without awkwardness in public places is provided. Case material and examples are used extensively so you will get models for practice in these areas.

The remaining pages give information regarding further study and training in pastoral practice. The epilogue is an appeal for you to continue with confidence your much needed pastoral practice in everyday places.

## 32. Leading to Insight

Nobody likes to have his or her nose rubbed in anything disagreeable. One's shortcomings are execrably disagreeable. "Giving" insight is nose-rubbing. Leading to insight is an art or craft that is simple to suggest, difficult to master.

The reason leading to insight is difficult to master is that we usually want to aggrandize our own egos. Rubbing people's noses is a simple and quick way to make one feel smart, superior, successful—even if the consultee whose nose we rub is not benefited.

Leading to insight is a slow, painful, often unrewarding process. The consultee usually benefits, however. A typical choice confronting the consultant is that between telling someone what her or his problem is, or setting and resetting the "stage" for him or her to discover (when emotionally "ready") his or her own "growing edge." Consultation is a bit like "teaching" someone to swim or ride a bicycle. All the advice, direction, illustration, analogy, and exhortation in one's vocabulary are so much "blowing in the wind."

Learning to lead to insight requires a giving up of the very human desire to aggrandize the self at the expense of consultees. Those who realize that they are worthwhile human beings apart from "telling" (telling off?) consultees, who realize they are capable of patience, setbacks, tolerance, the ability to "live and let live," can learn to lead to insight.

Leading to insight is the appropriately timed juxtaposing of two facts in such a way as to make possible a linking into a "cause-and-effect" conclusion by consultees when they are ready emotionally. No complicated case histories are needed to make sense of the following contrasting "giving insight" versus "leading to insight" statements.

*A giving-insight statement:*
> "What's wrong with you is that you're afraid to leave Momma!"

*The same insight presented in a leading way:*
> "Your mother keeps you from having a life of your own, but you cannot afford to move to an apartment or rooming house?"

*Giving:*
> "Having a sick wife makes you feel healthy!"

*Leading:*
> "Your wife is emotionally ill, but you wouldn't want to offend her by consulting a psychiatrist?"

99

*Giving:*

> "If you *really* wanted to get out of debt you'd cut up your credit cards fast—don't try to kid me!"

*Leading:*

> "You'd like to get out of debt but you feel you can't just cut up all your credit cards?"

*Giving:*

> "You like to suffer—martyr-marriage is what you want!"

*Leading:*

> "You're in a miserable marriage that you can't tolerate, yet you still believe divorce is immoral?"

*Giving:*

> "If you *really* wanted friends, you'd join every club going and jump into group therapy!"

*Leading:*

> "You say you want desperately to have friends, but you feel you are not interested in a social club or therapy group?"

*Giving:*

> "Your problem is you enjoy the shame of being fat!"

*Leading:*

> "You know you are unable to diet on your own, but you feel that joining a weight-control group or placing yourself under a physician's supervision is a cop out?"

*Giving:*

> "You don't really want to find the right girl or you'd attend the church's singles group—don't try to kid me!"

*Leading:*

> "You say you want to meet a nice girl and get married, but think you'd be bored by the church's singles group?"

Giving insight is the equivalent in one form or another of "telling (off)" people, "You enjoy suffering!" which none of us care to hear. Few of us will admit enjoying suffering, unless, of course, we wish to prove the "accuser" correct. That is a symptom of not being emotionally ready to constructively use insight.

Once in a great while a consultant may wish to precipitate a crisis in a person's life for the person's own good (not the consultant's) and a little nose-rubbing may be beneficial. Such should only be undertaken when one is fully ready to cope with the possible results (which may include suicidal or homicidal attempts, even on the life of the consultant)—and under competent supervision.

For example, I was approached by a consultee who was on a collision course with personal tragedy. She was an unusually attractive young woman who had taken up the habit of frequenting low-class bars late at night, flirting with drunken, obviously disreputable men, then leaving alone and walking through dreary streets and dimly lit alleys, self-destructively exposing herself to assault. She had consistently refused to reveal this behavior to her psychiatrist.

On a morning I knew she was *en route* for an appointment with her doctor, she consulted me in a parking lot. I told her, with full awareness of the dangers involved, what I thought.

"I think you are hell-bent on getting yourself raped again, and that you so despise yourself that you secretly hope to be killed in a cruel, disfiguring way. That's why you do such dangerous things."

She nodded agreement in a sophisticated way, thanked me politely for my opinion, went on to her appointment, and voluntarily admitted herself to a psychiatric hospital. She has not spoken to me for over five years, but is now happily married and successfully pursuing a dual career as mother and respected professional person in a city a thousand miles away.

Such nose-rubbing is a dangerous and delicate tool to be used sparingly. Such high-risk efforts should be attempted only for the consultee's eventual benefit, never to make the consultant feel better.

## 33. The Gain Question
## or "How do you avoid getting what you want?"

There are two kinds of questions that sooner or later hit "pay dirt" in consultation. One is the Gain question. It goes like this:

"What are the gains you get from having this problem?" Thirty percent of the time people will thereby be led to insight and respond with enlightenment that sets them to reconsideration of their style of life. The other seventy percent of the time people will blink and say they do not gain anything, what do you mean, etc.

Soft-hearted consultants will respond with a rephrasing of the question in some manner such as, "I mean, what is the result of your continuing problem in this area?"

Forty percent of the time people will then say something like, "Oh, well, I guess I end up hurting, again." To this the consultant replies, "Yes, that's what I thought you were gaining from this—pain." This is followed by juxtaposition of statements as discussed in the preceding section.

Thirty percent of the people will still not get the point and will Declare this openly—"I can't understand what you mean. I guess I'm too dumb to." This usually means they are not ready for the insight emotionally.

It is a good thing we can be patient and let live.

A second kind of question, usually directed at those who lament not getting what they profess to want from life, is some variation of the basic formula, "How do you avoid getting what you want?" Half of the people to whom I address this question answer immediately, usually with a mirthless laugh of some sort.

Most of us have a fairly sophisticated comprehension of the process by which we go about *not* getting what we want. (Try this one on yourself for a few minutes—no surprise.)

The other half of the people I ask this process question respond with something like, "I'm not sure I know what you mean. Will you explain it to me?"

The correct answer to such a request is to say, "No. Now tell me how you avoid getting what you want." Forty percent do so. The other ten percent are not ready.

This is not nose-rubbing. Many of us, once we realize the process by which we do what we do, are rather proud of our ingenuity. Further, if the question has been asked as a request for information rather than a condemnation, the consultee may reconsider what she or he really *does* want. We often prefer "those ills we have than fly to others we know not of." Once we realize this we may not have a problem.

Insight into what people gain from having their specific problems and comprehending how they avoid getting what they want is the essence of the work of consultation. "When we are aware of what we are doing, we are cured" is a slogan of Gestaltists. "To know what you are doing is the opposite of being scripted" is Berne's way of putting it.

When I know what I am doing and getting from doing that, I can choose whether or not to continue. I can decide whether or not the gain is what I want to continue to gain. I may have the same behavior, the same symptoms, the same "problems," but I have them by choice. I am "master" rather than slave of my emotional embroilments.

We may wonder why people remain in painful circumstances, keep abusing themselves emotionally, even after they know what they are doing, realize that their gains are pain and hurt. People usually will tell you if you ask.

"The reason I stay married to that no-good and put up with all these problems is because I'd rather do that than be alone," one woman said.

A young man stated: "I know I feel terrible when I take my anger out on myself, when I get depressed. That is the only time I feel anything, however. I'd rather be depressed than numb. I don't feel like a person unless I'm feeling something. And pain seems to be what I can feel most readily."

One middle-aged man answered the question as follows: "Getting drunk is how I avoid attaining the achievements I say I want. Drinking makes me non-productive. I guess secretly I am still resisting all the pushing to achieve

I've had from childhood. If I do not achieve while sober, I can't stand the guilt. So I drink and my drinking buddies like me for who I am, not because I've achieved something."

The following is a verbatim account of a conversation with a young man who said he was depressed "all the time" because he wanted to be creative, be an artist, and an actor, rather than "continue at my dull grind job with the company."

*Consultant:* What you really want is to get rid of your uninspiring job and get into art and the theater.

*Young Man:* Yes, definitely. I drag to work every day. I hate what I do. The money is not all that good. I get home at night feeling empty and depressed. Life seems meaningless.

*Consultant:* And you want to get out of all that and get into creativity?

*Young Man:* [wistfully] I sure do.

*Consultant:* What do you gain from staying where you are?

*Young Man:* Huh? Did you say gain? Well, [mirthless chuckle] nothing, except misery. No. There's no gain for me. What did you ask?

*Consultant:* You answered me. I asked what you gain from staying where you are and you answered that you gain misery.

*Young Man:* Ha. But why would anyone want to stay miserable? I mean, nobody likes to be unhappy. I certainly don't like to be unhappy. Ha.

*Consultant:* You want to be happy, to work in art and acting?

*Young Man:* [surprised pause] Why, ah, I guess by staying in my present job. I sure stay unhappy there. But you can't just quit your job, not just to go try to be happy. And besides, what if I don't really have any talent? I mean I do have responsibilities down there. I wouldn't feel right just up and quitting. And I've no idea how to begin, where to begin looking for . . . Believe me, I'm not trying to stay unhappy. I mean, you seem to think that I *want* to stay unhappy. I really don't. [thoughtful pause]

*Consultant:* It's OK for you to take your time finding your way into art and the theater. You can keep the security of your job until you know your way around in the art world and so on.

*Young Man:* I guess I'm a little afraid of leaving my job. As much as I hate it, I do know I can do the work. Maybe I could stay on there and I know some people at the Art Academy. I could get into a night course there and *see* how it goes.

*Consultant:* Would you feel a little more fulfilled if you did start slowly, gradually check things out?

*Young Man:* Yeah. Doing both wouldn't be bad. But it's hard to believe I want to be unhappy. I guess I do want the security, but not the unhappiness.

*Consultant:* I didn't say you wanted to be unhappy. I asked how you avoided getting the happiness and fulfillment you say you want. You said by staying with your present job. You also said you'd be happier by gradually getting into art and so on. Sounds like you've come up with a pretty good plan.

*Young Man:* Yeah—now if I just follow the plan!

*Consultant:* How might you avoid following the plan?

*Young Man:* [delightful laugh] By standing and talking to you here all day instead of calling Nan over at the Art Academy. Thanks! See you later.

## *34. Crisis Consultation (Emergencies* Emerge*)*

There is a difference between crisis consultation (or "intervention" as such is commonly called) and most other kinds of consulting. The differences are essentially two.

First, people in crisis who appeal for help are almost always truly wanting a specific kind of help. They are seldom "playing games" in the popular sense of the expression. They are in a "dependent" position. They range from those who are extremely anxious to those in outright panic. What they seek is almost always the same specific type of help.

This specific type of help is summed up in a single word—alternatives. People in crisis seek alternatives to the usual way by which they cope with problems. Most of us have habitual ways of coping with problems. These include losing our temper, withdrawing from persons or problems, denial that there is a problem, and attempts to manipulate. When these devices fail, are overwhelmed by crisis, we regress to childlike dependence on others for alternative ways to cope.

Second, people in true crisis usually welcome and act upon viable alternatives provided in appropriate ways.

Some people seem always in crisis. Some seem to have five emergencies at once. Such people are not truly in crisis. They are in some form of rather stereotyped, "scripted," repetitive behavior. They usually do not seem to appreciate our help. As Perls says, "true emergencies *emerge*" above the melodramatic landscape of "chronic crisis" life-styles.

Several excellent resources are available regarding general crisis intervention procedures, such as *The Minister as Crisis Counselor* by David Switzer (Nashville: Abingdon, 1974) as well as more general works included in the general bibliography.

The following case illustrations demonstrate elementary principles for consultation in specifically psychiatric crises:

104

The Reverend Mr. B., an assistant pastor in a 1000-member church, telephoned the state hospital chaplain one evening. He said, "A woman talked with me at a garage where we were both getting our automobiles serviced this morning. Her conversation was not quite coherent, but her distress was obvious. I urged her to see her doctor. Just a few minutes ago she telephoned me at home saying all kinds of strange things. She was crying and begged me to come to her apartment. She said her doctor is out of the city for the day and that I was her only hope. I told her I would go see her, but I'm not sure what to say or do. Would you accompany me?" The chaplain agreed to do so.

The woman, Mrs. M., was about forty years old, and very thin. When the pastors arrived, she was talking with a woman in a neighboring apartment. Mrs. M. immediately began talking rapidly and fearfully. Her pastor interrupted to perform appropriate introductions, and asked if they might move to her apartment to talk. There Mrs. M. told of having seen and heard her dead mother speaking in the apartment. "Then, right before I telephoned you," she said, "I had all kinds of strange experiences. My body got very cold. I thought I was dying . . . and I heard music, strange music . . . they said my mother would not have died if I had taken better care of her . . . my husband is not here . . . we're divorced . . . I had to quit my job . . . my hands are not so cold now . . . does that mean I'm going to live?"

The chaplain asked Mrs. M., "What did you think of doing when you were so frightened?"

"I called the minister. But he, you, were so long getting here, that I finally ran to the lady next door. I had to get to people. I go there often. We drink coffee and talk." Mrs. M. gradually became more calm and coherent. She told of her lonely life since her mother's death four years before, of her divorce from her husband, and of giving up her job recently.

The chaplain asked about her sleep and appetite. She said she had not slept well for several months, and had taken no food except coffee in the past day or two. Then she asked if the ministers would pray with her and for her.

"Certainly, but in addition to prayer, I think you should see a doctor as soon as you can," the chaplain replied. "We can drive you to a hospital tonight."

"No, I think I can make it alone tonight," she said. "I have an appointment for ten o'clock in the morning, with my doctor."

"Well," the chaplain replied, "if you become very frightened, call this number" (he wrote the number of the local general hospital emergency room), "and ask for the doctor. If necessary, they will send an ambulance or police car. You can get medicine at the hospital and maybe stay, maybe come back. If you don't get upset again, you can wait until morning and see your own doctor or call the city mental health clinic" (writing this number also).

Mrs. M. agreed with this, and after a prayer "for courage in lonely and frightening times," the pastors left. They had stayed about forty minutes.

Mrs. M. received medication the following day from her family physician. She also made an appointment with the community mental health center, where she later joined in group therapy. She regularly attended Sunday worship, and has been employed for the past four years. Her physical and mental condition appear greatly improved.

Comment: Mrs. M. was obviously in acute distress. She believed herself to hear voices, see the dead walking, and felt her own death at hand. Her physical appearance was bad, and she could neither eat nor sleep. No formal acquaintance with psychiatric subtleties was necessary to suspect that Mrs. M. was mentally ill. The question the pastor faced was whether she should be taken to a hospital immediately, or whether she could wait and carry out the plans she had made with her family physician. The pastoral decision was to let Mrs. M. decide. One reason the chaplain trusted her was because of her reaction under severe stress. She turned toward other people when in difficulty. Had she locked the door, withdrawn from people, turned against or away from others, the chaplain would have felt strongly the need to seek hospitalization. As it was, despite her acute suffering and fearful distress, the visit of the pastors and her own inclination to seek help from people indicated Mrs. M.'s ability to continue in her own way toward a return of health, even in what seemed a psychiatric crisis.

Mr. W., a middler seminarian and weekend student pastor, telephoned his professor of pastoral care one night:

"Professor, I am at the home of parishioners. Mrs. C. and her children have come here. They say that Mr. C., a deacon in my church, who has been treated in a psychiatric hospital in the past, chased them from their house. He has been drinking and he has a gun. He has fired the gun in the house several times. We're afraid he might hurt himself or someone else. We cannot talk to his doctor until tomorrow. He warned the family not to go near the house. Now, should I go over there and try to talk with him?"

The professor suggested that the family consider taking out a mental inquest warrant and have the police transport Mr. C. to the city general hospital; also that the student pastor accompany the family but let them sign the warrant. The professor gave the student the telephone number of the city hospital, and the name of the psychiatric resident in charge. By calling him, the family learned the necessary steps to take in having Mr. C. hospitalized. He was evaluated at the hospital, and discharged the following day with follow-up plans for treatment. Two and a half years later no repetition of such an incident had occurred. Mr. C. has been getting along well with the family and in the church.

Comment: Pastors are seldom trained to deal with threatening persons, let alone to disarm them. Police and other peace officers are usually trained for such emergencies, and should be called on. Pastors, ordinarily, should not assume responsibilities which are properly the family's or the law enforcement agencies' any more than they should perform surgery or pave streets. They can and should be familiar with appropriate resources for any emergency, advise and assist families in making constructive decisions, and remain "with" families and individuals under stress. If the pastor feels she or he must be involved directly, she or he should seek the advice of a physician and/or attorney. Ideally, not the pastor, but the congregation, through their duly elected representatives, should corporately take action when there is no responsible family. If the sick person has no family to help him or her, he or she should be able to depend on the church-family.

A young minister, the Reverend Mr. T., followed the results of a city-wide religious census by personally calling on all non-churched persons near his church. In an obviously expensive older house, he was greeted by Mr. S., a sixty-eight-year-old successful salesperson, and a bachelor. Mr. T. had been introduced to him once about a year before. Mr. S. invited the minister in, then paced the floor frantically, talking rapidly and loudly. He said he was ill, that he had flu, and that he was going to have a stroke and die. He felt the world was coming to its end. He said he could neither sleep, work, nor eat ("only tea and cigars, and not an hour of sleep in five days"). The man broke into sobs, embracing the young minister, and shouting, "What can I do? What's going to happen? Help me!"

The minister timidly inquired about family. "None!" snorted the other, resuming his pacing. "I stayed here with mother until she died seventeen years ago. Now I have no one." The man began to wail and sob again.

The minister asked Mr. S. if he had consulted a physician. Mr. S. stopped pacing to explain that his mother had been a Christian Scientist, and he had almost never been to a doctor. "A doctor could not help me anyway," he continued. "I'm going to die and the world is ending. Won't you, a person of God, do something?" The minister told Mr. S., "I do not see how you can continue to suffer this way, and I will do what I can to help. But I believe you ought to see a doctor. It shouldn't make you feel any worse, and it could help."

Mr. S. said he did not know any doctors. The pastor said he could suggest a doctor if Mr. S. was willing to talk to him by telephone. Mr. S., after further weeping, consented. The minister phoned the office of the town's only psychiatrist, Dr. B. He explained to the nurse who he was, and said, "I think the man I'm with should talk with Dr. B. right away." The nurse said this was impossible but if the minister could get Mr. S. to the office, the doctor could see him. The minister then let Mr. S. talk with the nurse. He agreed to accompany the minister to the office.

On arrival, and after a bad moment when Mr. S. realized Dr. B. was a psychiatrist, they entered the office. The waiting room was crowded, which seemed to comfort Mr. S. He and the pastor talked at length, about business, sports, and travel. Then the doctor saw Mr. S. for ten minutes. Mr. S. emerged from the office, angry.

"That guy wants to stick me in a hospital," he shouted. He paid his bill while the psychiatrist told the minister, "Try to get him to the hospital." The pastor drove Mr. S. to his home, doubtful if Mr. S. would ever consent to hospitalization.

Mr. S. called the pastor about 11:30 at night from the city bus station. He said he was having an attack, adding, "I think I'm dying."

The pastor said, "I could not get to you in less than an hour. You call the police or someone there to help you. Give them my number. Maybe this is what Dr. B. feared. Maybe this is why he wanted you hospitalized."

Mr. S. called again at two o'clock in the morning. "I'm home now, but I'm worse. Do you think Dr. B. will still let me in the hospital?" The pastor said he thought so. "Well, I'll call him now and start packing. If you can drive me there about 8:00 A.M., I'll pay you. I could get a taxi, but I don't want to go in alone." Mr. T. said he would be at Mr. S.'s home at eight the next morning.

Mr. S. called again at 6:00 A.M. "I'm packed, but sinking fast. Maybe I'd better just die here like mother. I'll never make it 'til eight o'clock." Mr. T. assured Mr. S. he would come immediately, and did so.

After several last-minute hesitations, the pastor got Mr. S. to the hospital. Dr. B. had given instructions and treatment began at once.

The pastor visited Mr. S., conferred with Dr. B., and three weeks later drove the patient home. He said he felt "like a different person." Mr. S. did not attend Mr. T.'s church regularly, but progressively improved. Five years later when visiting as a house guest of the pastor (who had moved to a distant city), Mr. S. boasted of having received the company award as top salesperson for the last two years. Mr. S. continues to function at a high level as he approaches his seventy-sixth year.

Comment: The Reverend Mr. T. was unexpectedly confronted by a near stranger who apparently had no family or friends to rely on when he became seriously distressed. He did several things that were apparently helpful. He became a concerned friend, yet (and this is important) did not force his advice or help on Mr. S.

Mr. T. made suggestions yet permitted Mr. S. to remain responsible for himself, and make the final decisions about seeing a doctor and hospitalization. Mr. T. did not seem compelled to override Mr. S.'s autonomy. He was honest, made suggestions, and left his telephone number. Then Mr. S. called on Mr. T. for help.

If Mr. S. had not done so, Mr. T. could have kept in communication, by telephone and/or visit, still permitting Mr. S. some responsibility for himself. If severe crisis developed, there are always the police. Yet the communication of continuing concern and availability almost always gives distressed persons sufficient time, courage, and support to decide responsibly for their own best interests.

Finally, it might have seemed more dramatic had the pastor driven to the bus station in the middle of the night, in answer to Mr. S.'s call. Yet such removing of self-responsibility could have been resented by Mr. S., leading him to feel that he was not trusted. It probably would have delayed hospitalization. Mr. T., without backing down in his conviction that Mr. S. needed professional help in addition to pastoral care, still communicated concern, and gave Mr. S. further opportunity to help himself.

### *Conclusions*

Four factors are significant in these case illustrations:

1. Professional *assistance* was sought from others in every instance. These pastors did not feel that they alone should handle what to them were psychiatric crises. They had the security of accepting their limitations and could consult with others without feeling that their professional identity and status were being threatened. Someone has said there are three times when assistance is imperative:

a. when you are not sure what is going on within a person or situation.

b. when you are aware of what is at hand and know you are not adequately trained to cope with the situation; or,

c. when you are personally and emotionally involved to such a degree that your ability to be objective and employ clear judgment is impaired (as with your family or close personal friends or a parishioner toward whom you have especially strong feelings of affection, anger, etc.).

2. *Continued* communication of concern and care was evident in each instance, as consultation and referral took place. As Wayne Oates once phrased it, "referral is not ditching." The pastor continues appropriate visits and sharing throughout referrals, keeping in communication with all concerned. (In rare instances it may not help a psychiatric patient to see the pastor for a brief time, but the psychiatrist is the one to make this decision. The pastor can still visit with the family.)

3. *Respect* for persons. In each case the pastor demonstrated respect for the "responsible-ness" of persons involved. In the instance of Deacon C., with his

loaded revolver, the pastor encouraged the family to take appropriate actions. He could have taken action himself ("Well, I saved the town from a maniac last night") but did not. He helped the family through the painful process of swearing out a warrant. Thus they could later feel that they, not the pastor, had "done what was necessary." Perhaps Mr. C. later appreciated the fact that his own family, not relative strangers, had so looked after him.

4. *Companionship* was provided for the disturbed persons. "The real evil in mental disorder is not to be found in the conflict, but in the sense of isolation or estrangement." These pastors relied heavily on the belief that to keep people in communication with other people is to keep hope alive. Where companionship breaks down, so do we.

## 35. *Professional Confidentiality*

We borrow from the Reality Therapists a key word for consideration of professional confidentiality—responsibility. The professional consultant is responsible in all her or his life. This, put into practical language, means that the consultant does not guarantee anyone "secret" deals. Aside from the Seal of the Confessional, consultants do not agree to secretiveness. They agree to handle responsibly anything they may learn from or about a consultee.

Many people "put to the test" a consultant by making such requests as, "You do promise that you'll never under any circumstances reveal what I'm about to tell you?"

The correct response to such requests is something like, "I promise I will not use anything you tell me to hurt you—but I will not give you a guarantee of secrecy. For all I know you may be bout to tell me that you intend to murder someone else or yourself. If that were the case, I'd take any needed action to protect you from such a disaster."

Should the consultee then respond, "Well, in that case, I won't tell you what I wanted to tell you," the consultant can comfortably say, "Perhaps you'd better not, unless you can trust me whether I make promises or not. The point in our relationship is not what I promise, but whether or not you trust me."

In over twenty years as a professional consultant with people whose stations in life have ranged from high-ranking public officials to "Forensic Unit" psychiatric patients, only once has a consultee refused to "tell" what he had to say. I later learned, by odd chance, that his secret was that at times he doubted the divinity of Christ. I have the feeling that he would return to consult with me if anything of more earthly danger were on his mind.

The consultant never wants to compromise himself or herself in such a way as to be unable ethically to intervene in irrevocable matters of life and death. Should a consultee divulge the fact that she or he has a gun and intends to kill someone, the consultant should not be in a relationship so "confidential" that she or he cannot get to a telephone, call, and give warning.

Responsible relationships spell professional confidentiality. Secret conversations do not.

## 36. Religion or Sickness?

At times the matters about which a consultant is consulted may seem strange. The unusual or even bizarre may initially seem like severe sickness of the mind. Often the consultee feels he or she is undergoing a religious experience, but may seem to be in a "psychotic episode." How is the consultant to determine the difference?

Since the early published work of Anton Boisen, we have known that the distinction between religion and sickness lies, not in the immediate expressions of a person, but in the long-range outcome. When the long-range outcome is destructive to self and others, alienates, isolates, and culminates in the termination of helpful communication and the dilapidation of an individual's personality, that is sickness.

When the long-range outcome is increased community, even after turmoil and crisis, enhancement of "fullness of life" for the person and others, and an increase in the "general welfare," that is religious experience.

Looking for the "fruits of the Spirit" beneath and beyond the immediate helps the consultant to determine the difference.

A college girl said to her father: "I know I have been brought up in a Christian home, but I have never had a conversion experience. I have been told that I can't really be a Christian unless I have had a moving spiritual experience."

The swaying revival crowd, the evangelist's oratory, "speaking in tongues," emotional ecstasy, and "convicted sinners" streaming down aisles are not always the "fruits of the Spirit" of the New Testament. "Love, joy, peace, patience, kindness, goodness, faithfulness, gentleness, self-control" are. (Gal. 5:22–23)

A patient in a mental hospital said: "Last night I saw God glowing in the darkness. He told me to die for the sins of the world." Her doctor advised her to remain in the hospital for treatment. A week later she reported a similar experience, saying, "God wants me to preach all over the world." The psychiatrist repeated his advice. Two weeks later she said: "I saw God again last night.

He told me that my family need me." The doctor said: "And soon you should be leaving the hospital. I hope you will remember us here in your prayers." He recognized the Spirit of God at work, even in her delusions.

Few of us have such excessive emotional experiences. But where the qualities or fruits of the Spirit are present, there we detect the true Spirit of God.

What shall the consultant do when confronted by a person who may be deeply enmeshed in an ecstatic religious experience or the grip of an attack of mental illness? Following the example set by our Lord and the experience of specialists in working with the mentally ill is almost always helpful.

The first healing by Jesus recorded in Luke is of a man apparently mentally ill. Occasionally in a mental hospital chapel service, some worshiper rises to speak at an inappropriate time. The trained hospital chaplain knows that there are two essentials if the unauthorized speaker is to be spared embarrassment and the worship is not to be destructively disrupted.

The first essential is communication of God's respect and love for people. The second is a sense of firmness that is not "bossy."

Jesus communicated these essentials and the man was apparently reassured. It is impossible to imagine Jesus responding in any other way. We cannot picture him saying, "Somebody get that nut out of here!" It is inconceivable that he would shout "You sit down, you idiot, or I'll force you to!" Respect and God's firm love gave the man a sense of acceptance and security.

Most of us have evidenced times of frustration, anxiety, and despair, whether diagnosed as mental illness or not. Reassurance of God's interest in us and the security of God's firm love bring healing to us.

Further operational procedures for consultants have been outlined in chapter 34.


## 37. Value Systems and Consultation—"Prophetic Ministry"

A major problem confronting consultants is that of knowing how far to go in accepting the attitudes and actions of consultees whose value systems are different from the consultant's. To state the dilemma another way, "How do I determine the line between acceptance of a person and condoning attitudes and actions of which I do not approve?"

Each consultant will, of course, have to make this decision in each specific situation. There can be no timeless rules or regulations that will always take the responsibility for ethical decision and behavior off the back of the consultant. Flexibility and a willingness to reconsider one's own values are a part of the Judeo-Christian heritage, especially for post-Reformation Protestants, and post-Vatican II Roman Catholics.

The decision in each situation must also be based on the long-term welfare of the consultee and society, not the prejudices or personal predilections of the consultant.

Since the 1960s most contemporary clergy have experienced the impressive force of the change in divorce attitudes by society generally and even the most conservative of churches in the United States. There was a time in this consultant's experience when, generally speaking, the welfare of people and society was best served by preserving all but the most viciously bad marriages. That time has passed. The increased emancipation of women, the social acceptableness of single-parent children, and the modernization of divorce laws in most states have led to increased realization that often the best interest of parents, children, and society are served by "good" divorce counseling more than continuing failures to make incipiently bad marriages better.

The consultant should always be prepared to refer those whose attitudes and actions are not "condonable" by her or him to some other qualified expert who can ethically work with such persons. The consultant's task *in his or her role as consultant,* is not to *try* to change people who do not wish to change morally. But, in the role of prophetic preacher or social activist or evangelist, he or she may make every effort to do so. The rehabilitation systems of correctional facilities may, and should, do so. But, *as consultant,* she or he should not "cross transactions" or "mix apples with oranges," by offering that which the consultee does not want (or perhaps even need).

One of the most expert consultants I know spends a lot of time working with extremely conservative people. He repeatedly works with them in personal matters, helpfully. He also repeatedly urges that they read articles, attend lectures, and visit "liberal" church worship services to help them re-examine their "secret gun club mentality" of which he does not approve.

Competent consultants do not compromise their convictions, but neither do they coerce consultees with their own value systems. Nor do they conceal the beliefs by which they live when to do so would be dishonest to themselves and/or their consultees.


## 38. Consultation and Evangelism

The most effective evangelism has always been the providing of what people need in a way they can accept without feeling dehumanized. In some instances this is accomplished by a simple telling of the Good News to people who want to hear—as Paul did on Mars Hill. In other times bread to the hungry and drink to the thirsty is Good News.

When the consultant effectively provides that which people want and need, directly or indirectly, the Good News is sown. Some does fall on poor soil and gives no yield—for a time at least. But very often, those who are helped demonstrate their appreciation by supporting the work of the church in a variety of ways.

One example of this was the three-year experience of a young pastor in a church with a small membership and an aggressive Evangelism Committee. The young pastor, with such a small congregation, was able to spend considerable time visiting in local nursing homes, the county hospital, serving on various community organizations, etc. At the end of three years, thirty new members had united with that congregation—four as a result of the efforts of the Evangelism Committee, twenty-six as a result of assistance the pastor and church had been able to offer those whose first contact with the church was through consulting with the young pastor.

In short, competent consultation *is* effective evangelism!

## 39. Prayer and Consultation

The consultant may be called upon for prayer in public settings. Our first impulse is to quote Jesus' comment: "And when thou prayest, thou shalt not be as the hypocrites are: for they love to pray standing . . . in the corners of the streets."

However, some people do really want the reassurance of our prayers. The most non-hypocritical way to honor this request is to (1) determine that is what people *really* want—i.e. they are not just saying that to get rid of us or to show respect for our cloth; (2) ask specifically what they wish included in the prayer; (3) offer what has been called an "open-eyed" prayer.

An "open-eyed" prayer is one in which the consultant looks at the consultee and states clearly exactly what he or she will be praying.

"Mr. Smith, I assure you that I will be praying that your wife shall come through her surgery with a minimum of pain or fear, and that she will be healed completely this time."

Or, "I know you have done everything you know to help your son, and my prayer for you is that you will feel comforted as he seeks his own way, and not feel that you are losing him because he is not going to follow his dad's footsteps." Etc.

Prayer should *not* be the occasion for trying to push insights or club people with truths they are not ready emotionally to receive. Prayer should be directed to God with people, not at people for "God's" (our) sake.

Prayer with people should be agreed to when people sincerely request it, not when we feel stumped as to what to do or say next.

In the privacy of our own hearts and thoughts, we can always pray and often need to pray, if we are to consult effectively. In a sense through prayer, God is the Great Consultant for us all.

114

## 40. What Else Can I Learn and Where?

The ideas and exercises suggested in this book are but an introduction to consultation. You need to read at least everything in the bibliography of this book.

You also need accredited supervision in clinical practice. Information for this may be obtained from a Teaching Fellow of the American Association of Pastoral Counselors, a Supervisor of the Association for Clinical Pastoral Education, a Clinical Teaching Member of the International Transactional Analysis Association, or a Board certified psychiatrist or psychoanalyst, or an accredited clinical psychologist.

Competent supervision, group and individual, is imperative if one is to attain ability to help anyone anywhere. Ordinarily, a secondary "union card" is essential if one hopes to consult for "profit." A degree in clinical psychology, becoming a licensed or registered nurse, becoming a mental health technician, securing a masters in social work, a teacher's certificate, a Master of Divinity or Doctor of Medicine or membership in the bar are primary ways for becoming a consultant in the professional sense. Housewives, butchers, friendly neighbors, automobile mechanics, door-to-door salespersons, pharmacists, deliverypersons, or bartenders can consult effectively, if financial gain, specifically from consulting, is not a necessary consideration. I know one door-to-door cosmetic salesperson who spent considerable time consulting with her many customers in their homes. The cosmetic orders she sold on these visits were all but incidental to the help she provided more often than not.

Certified or accredited supervision during the learning phase of consultation is essential, except for the very few who know themselves extraordinarily well, and who can master the elementary principles outlined in this book without resort to supervision and/or therapy.

You can obtain the addresses of the nearest qualified training centers from the following:

American Association of Pastoral Counselors, Inc.,
3 West 29th Street,
New York, NY 10001

Association for Clinical Pastoral Education, Inc.,
Interchurch Center, Suite 450, 475 Riverside Drive,
New York, NY 10027

International Transactional Analysis Association,
1772 Vallejo Street,
San Francisco, CA 94123

American Psychiatric Association,
1700 Eighteenth Street, NW,
Washington, DC 20009

You can also contact the nearest medical or mental teaching hospital chaplains department, psychology department of a college or university, ATS accredited theological seminary, or private practitioners who have authentic credentials.

# Epilogue

Once you have mastered the material in this book, not just intellectually, but emotionally and pragmatically, you will probably find that your pastoral practice in everyday places will be curtailed.

The reason is that people will sense your competence and expertise. They will no longer approach you in supermarket aisles and barnyards with problems. They will, instead, ask you for an appointment in your office. Once people *know* that *you* are *the* One, they will not settle for snatched seconds in secular situations. They will demand a special time and place for their deeper concerns.

What you start out to do is practice consultation with anyone anywhere. In time, office practice will encroach on your time to the exclusion of your doing so.

Nevertheless, the rich rewards of continuing your pastoral practices in everyday places are many. They include increased self-confidence, enriched spiritual and interpersonal experience, and stronger service more ably given, in the places to which we are called, among those to whom we have been sent.

# Bibliography

Ackerman, Nathan W. *The Psychodynamics of Family Life.* New York: Basic Books, 1958.

Adorno, Theodor W. *The Authoritarian Personality.* New York: Harper & Brothers, 1950.

Alexander, Franz. "Social Significance of Psychoanalysis and Psychotherapy." *Archives of General Psychiatry,* September 1954, pp. 235–244.

American Psychiatric Association. *Diagnostic and Statistic Manual of Mental Disorders.* Washington: American Psychiatric Association, 1968.

Angyal, Andras. *Neurosis and Treatment: A Holistic Theory.* New York: J. Wiley & Sons, 1965.

Arieti, Silvano, ed. *American Handbook of Psychiatry.* New York: Basic Books, 1959. 2d ed., rev., 1974.

Arnold, William Van, et al. *Divorce: Prevention or Survival?* Philadelphia: The Westminster Press, 1977.

Arnstein, Helene S. *What to Tell Your Child.* New York: Pocket Books, 1964.

Artiss, Kenneth L., and Bullard, Dexter M. "Paranoid Thinking in Everyday Life— The Function of Secrets and Disillusionment." *Academy of Medicine Bulletin* 11 (March 1965):57–63.

Bach, George, and Goldberg, Herb. *Creative Aggression.* New York: Avon Books, 1974.

Bach, George, and Wyden, Peter. *The Intimate Enemy.* New York: Avon Books, 1970.

Barton, Clarence Y., and Bennett, George F. "Communications: Breaking Bad News." *Journal of Pastoral Care* 19 (Winter 1965):231–233.

Baruch, Dorothy W. *New Ways in Discipline.* New York: Whittlesey House, 1949.

Bellak, Leopold, and Small, Leonard. *Emergency Psychotherapy and Brief Psychotherapy.* New York: Grune & Stratton, 1965.

Bennett, George F. "Pastoral Care in Psychiatric Crisis." *Pastoral Psychology,* June 1970, pp. 35–40.

———. "Religious Activity and the Suspicious Person." *Journal of Pastoral Care* 18 (Fall 1964):140–147.

———. "Spiritual Apathy: Some Causes and Cures for That Feeling of 'Couldn't Care Less'." *Presbyterian Life,* 15 August 1968.

———. "When Christians Meet Anger." *Presbyterian Life,* 15 September 1969.

Berne, Eric. *Games People Play*. New York: Grove Press, 1964.

―――. *A Layman's Guide to Psychiatry and Psychoanalysis*. New York: Grove Press, 1947.

―――. *Principles in Group Treatment*. New York: Oxford University Press, 1966.

―――. *Sex in Human Loving*. New York: Simon and Schuster, 1970.

―――. *Transactional Analysis in Psychotherapy*. New York: Grove Press, 1961.

―――. *What Do You Say after You Say Hello?* New York: Grove Press, 1972.

Bible, English. The Westminster Study Edition. Philadelphia: The Westminster Press, 1948.

Blackman, Nathan, et al. "The Sudden Murderer: Clues to Preventive Interaction." *Archives of General Psychiatry*, March 1963, pp. 289–294.

Boisen, Anton T. *The Exploration of the Inner World*. New York: Harper & Brothers, 1936.

Bonthius, Robert H. *Christian Paths to Self-Acceptance*. New York: King's Crown Press, 1948.

Bruder, Ernest E. "The Role of the Chaplain in Patient Relationships: Initial Religious Interview." *Journal of Pastoral Care* 7 (Spring 1953):37–41.

Buber, Martin. *I and Thou*. Translated by Ronald Gregor Smith. Edinburgh: T. & T. Clark, 1937.

Buhler, Charlotte. *Values in Psychotherapy*. New York: Free Press of Glencoe, 1962.

Cabot, Richard C., and Dicks, Russell L. *The Art of Ministering to the Sick*. New York: Macmillan, 1947.

Cameron, Norman. "Paranoid Conditions & Paranoia." *American Handbook of Psychiatry*. New York: Basic Books, 1959. Vol. I, pp. 508–539.

Cannon, Walter B. *The Wisdom of the Body*. New York: W. W. Norton & Co., 1963.

Caprio, Frank. *Marital Infidelity*. New York: Citadel, 1953.

Carson, Ira M., and Selsnick, Sheldon T. "Ego Strengthening Aspects of Supportive Psychotherapy." *American Journal of Psychotherapy* 13 (April 1959):298–318.

Cleckley, Hervey. *The Mask of Sanity*. St. Louis: Mosby, 1955.

―――. "Psychopathic States." *American Handbook of Psychiatry*. New York: Basic Books, 1959. Vol. I, pp. 567ff.

Clinebell, Howard J. *Basic Types of Pastoral Counseling*. Nashville: Abingdon, 1966.

Cousins, Ewert H., ed. *Process Theology*. New York: Paulist-Newman Press, 1971.

Darhonne, Allen. "Crisis: A Review of Theory and Research." *International Journal of Psychiatry* 13 (September 1965):371–384.

Dean, Edward S. "A Psychotherapeutic Investigation of Nagging." *Psychoanalytic Review* 51 (Winter 1964–65):555–561.

Deane, William N. "On Talking with the Deluded Schizophrenic Patient in Social Therapy." *Journal of Individual Psychology* 19 (November 1963):191–203.

DeRosis, Helen A., and Pellegrino, Victoria Y. *The Book of Hope: How Women Can Overcome Depression*. New York: Macmillan, 1976.

Draper, Edgar, et al. "On the Diagnostic Value of Religious Ideation." *Archives of General Psychiatry*, September 1965, pp. 202–207.

Dunbar, Helen Flanders, et al. *Mind and Body: Psychosomatic Medicine*. New York: Random House, 1955.

DuSay, John M. *Egograms*. New York: Harper & Row, 1977.

Ellis, Albert. *Humanistic Psychotherapy*. New York: McGraw-Hill Paperback Edition, 1974.

Ellis, Albert, and Harper, Robert A. *A New Guide to Rational Living*. Englewood Cliffs, N. J.: Prentice-Hall, 1975.

Erikson, Erik. *Childhood and Society.* New York: W. W. Norton & Co., 1950.

———. *Identity and the Life Cycle.* New York: International Universities Press, 1959.

Estes, H. R., et al. "Separation Anxiety." *American Journal of Psychotherapy* 10 (October 1956):682–695.

Fine, Reuben. "Erotic Feelings in the Psychotherapeutic Relationship." *Psychoanalytic Review,* Spring 1965, pp. 30–37.

Foulkes, S. H. *Therapeutic Group Analysis.* New York: International Universities Press, 1965.

Frank, Jerome D. *Persuasion and Healing.* Baltimore: Johns Hopkins Press, 1961.

Frankl, Viktor. *The Doctor and the Soul.* New York: Alfred A. Knopf, 1955.

Freedman, Alfred M.; Kaplan, Harold I.; and Sadock, Benjamin J. *Modern Synopsis of Comprehensive Textbook Psychiatry.* 2d ed. Baltimore: The Williams and Wilkins Co., 1976.

Freud, Sigmund. "Mourning and Melancholia." *Collected Papers.* London: Hogarth Press, 1950. Vol. IV.

———. *New Introductory Lectures on Psycho-Analysis.* New York: W. W. Norton & Co., 1965.

———. "Observations on Transference-Love." *Collected Papers.* London: Hogarth Press, 1950. Vol. II.

———. "Psycho-Analytic Notes upon an Autobiographical Account of a Case of Paranoia (Dementia Paranoides)" (1911). *Collected Papers.* London: Hogarth Press, 1950. Vol. III.

———. *The Psychopathology of Everyday Life.* New York: W. W. Norton & Co., 1971.

Friedman, Meyer, and Roseman, Ray H. *Type A Behavior and Your Heart.* Greenwich, Conn.: Fawcett, 1975.

Fromm, Erich. "Sex and Character." *The Dogma of Christ.* New York: Holt Rinehart & Winston, 1955. Pp. 107–130.

Fromm-Reichmann, Frieda. *Principles of Intensive Psychotherapy.* Chicago: University of Chicago Press, 1950.

Ginott, Haim, *Between Parent and Child.* New York: Macmillan, 1965.

Glasse, James D. *Profession: Minister.* Nashville: Abingdon, 1968.

———. *Putting It Together in the Parish.* Nashville: Abingdon, 1972.

Glasser, William. *Reality Therapy.* New York: Harper & Row, 1965.

Gordon, Thomas. *Parent Effectiveness Training.* New York: Plume Books, 1975.

Greenwald, Harold, ed. *Active Psychotherapy.* New York: Atherton Press, 1967.

———. "Treatment of the Psychopath." *Voices,* Spring 1967, pp. 50–61.

Haley, Jay. "Marriage Therapy." *Archives of General Psychiatry,* March 1963, pp. 213–234.

Haley, Jay, and Hoffman, Lynn. *Techniques of Family Therapy.* New York: Basic Books, 1967.

Harris, Thomas A. *I'm OK—You're OK.* New York: Harper & Row, 1967.

Hiltner, Seward. *Preface to Pastoral Theology.* New York: Abingdon, 1958.

———. *Theological Dynamics.* Nashville: Abingdon, 1972.

Hoch, Paul H., and Zubin, Joseph, eds. *Depression.* New York: Grune & Stratton, 1954.

Hollis, Florence. *Casework: Psychosocial Therapy.* New York: Random House, 1964.

Horkheimer, Max. "Authoritarianism in the Family." *The Family, Its Function and Destiny.* Edited by Ruth Anshen. New York: Harper & Row, 1959. Pp. 381–398.

Horney, Karen. *Feminine Psychology.* New York: W. W. Norton & Co., 1967.

———. *Neurosis and Human Growth.* New York: W. W. Norton & Co., 1950.

Irion, Paul. *The Funeral and the Mourners.* New York: Abingdon, 1954.

Jackson, Don D., ed. *Communication, Family, and Marriage.* Palo Alto, Calif.: Science and Behavior Books, 1968.

Jacobson, Gerald F. "Crisis Theory and Treatment Strategy: Some Sociocultural and Psychodynamic Considerations." *Journal of Nervous and Mental Disease* 141 (August 1965):209–218.

James, Muriel. *The Power at the Bottom of the Well.* New York: Harper & Row, 1974.

James, Muriel, and Jongeward, Dorothy. *Born to Win.* Reading, Mass.: Addison-Wesley, 1971.

James, William. *The Varieties of Religious Experience.* New York: Longmans, Green, and Co., 1902.

Johnson, Adelaide M. "Juvenile Delinquency." *American Handbook of Psychiatry.* New York: Basic Books, 1959. Vol. I, pp. 840ff.

Joint Committee on Worship. *The Worshipbook.* Philadelphia: The Westminster Press, 1970.

Jongeward, Dorothy, and Scott, Dru. *Affirmative Action for Women—A Practical Guide for Women and Management.* Reading, Mass.: Addison-Wesley, 1973.

Keen, Samuel. *Apology for Wonder.* New York: Harper & Row, 1969.

_____. *To a Dancing God.* New York: Harper & Row, 1970.

Kierkegaard, Søren. *Fear and Trembling.* London: Oxford University Press, 1939.

_____. *The Sickness unto Death.* Garden City, N. Y.: Doubleday Anchor Book, 1955.

Klink, Thomas. "The Chaplain and the Acutely Disturbed Patient." *Journal of Pastoral Care* 12 (Fall 1958):137–148.

Kopp, Sheldon B. *If You Meet the Buddha on the Road, Kill Him!* Ben Lomond, Calif.: Science and Behavior Books, 1972.

Laing, R. D. *The Politics of Experience.* New York: Ballantine Books, 1967.

Lake, Frank. *Clinical Theology.* London: Darton, Longman & Todd, 1966.

Langsley, Donald G., and Kaplan, David M. *The Treatment of Families in Crisis.* New York: Grune & Stratton, 1968.

Langsley, Pittman, Machotka, and Flonankealt. "Family Crisis Therapy—Results and Implications." *Family Process 7* (September 1968):145–158.

Lazarus, Arnold A. *Behavior Therapy and Beyond.* New York: McGraw-Hill, 1972.

Lederer, William J., and Jackson, Don D. *The Mirages of Marriage.* New York: W. W. Norton & Co., 1968.

Lowen, Alexander. *The Betrayal of the Body.* New York: Macmillan, 1969.

_____. *The Language of the Body.* New York: Macmillan, 1971.

_____. *Love and Orgasm.* New York: New American Library Signet Book, 1968.

Luther, Martin. *Table Talk.* New York: World Publishing Co., 1952.

MacDonald, Donald E. "Mental Disorders in the Wives of Alcoholics." *Quarterly Journal of the Studies of Alcoholism* 17 (June 1956):282–287.

Mandell, Arnold J. "The Fifteen Minute Hour." *Diseases of the Nervous System* 22 (October 1961):10.

Maslow, Abraham. *Motivation and Personality.* New York: Harper & Brothers, 1954.

Masters, William H., and Johnson, Virginia E. *Human Sexual Inadequacy.* Boston: Little, Brown & Co., 1970.

_____. *Human Sexual Response.* Boston: Little, Brown & Co., 1966.

May, Rollo. *The Meaning of Anxiety.* New York: Ronald Press Co., 1950.

Menninger, Karl; Mayman, Martin; and Pruyser, Paul. *The Vital Balance.* New York: Viking Press, 1963.

Messick, Henry (Hank). *Syndicate Wife.* New York: Macmillan, 1968.

Milton, John. "Lycidas." *The Complete Poetical Works of John Milton.* Boston: Houghton Mifflin Co., 1965.

Mowrer, O. H. *The Crisis in Psychiatry and Religion.* Princeton, N. J.: Van Nostrand, 1961.

Norris, Catherine H. "Psychiatric Crisis." *Perspectives in Psychiatric Care* 5 (1967): 20–28.

Oates, Wayne E. *Anxiety in Christian Experience.* Philadelphia: The Westminster Press, 1955.

———. *Christ and Selfhood.* New York: Association Press, 1961.

———. *The Christian Pastor.* Philadelphia: The Westminster Press, 1951.

———. *Protestant Pastoral Counseling.* Philadelphia: The Westminster Press, 1962.

———. *Religious Dimensions of Personality.* New York: Association Press, 1957.

Oates, Wayne E., and Neely, Kirk H. *Where to Go for Help.* Philadelphia: The Westminster Press, 1972.

Oden, Thomas C. *Contemporary Theology and Psychotherapy.* Philadelphia: The Westminster Press, 1972.

———. *Game Free.* New York: Dell Publishing Co., 1974.

O'Neill, Nena and George. *Open Marriage.* New York: M. Evans, 1972.

Outler, Albert C. *Psychotherapy and the Christian Message.* New York: Harper & Brothers, 1954.

Pattison, E. M. "Morality and the Treatment of the Character Disorders." *Journal of Religion and Health* 6 (October 1967):290–316.

Paul, Louis. "Crisis Intervention." *Mental Hygiene* 50 (January 1966):141–145.

Perls, Frederick S. (Fritz). *The Gestalt Approach and Eye Witness to Therapy.* Ben Lomond, Calif.: Science and Behavior Books, 1973.

———. *Gestalt Therapy Verbatim.* Lafayette, Calif.: Real People Press, 1969.

———. *In and Out of the Garbage Pail.* New York: Bantam Books, 1969.

Polster, Erving and Miriam. *Gestalt Therapy Integrated.* New York: Brunner/Mazel, 1973.

Powdermaker, Florence B., and Frank, Jerome D. *Group Psychotherapy: Studies in Methodology of Research and Therapy.* Cambridge, Mass.: Harvard University Press, 1953.

Puzo, Mario. *The Godfather.* Greenwich, Conn.: Fawcett, 1970.

Rado, Sandor. "The Border Region between the Normal and the Abnormal." *Ministry and Medicine in Human Relations.* Edited by Iago Galdston. New York: International Universities Press, 1955. Pp. 33–46.

Reeves, Robert B. "Non-Verbal Communication." *American Mental Hospital Chaplains Newsletter* 2 (1966):138–141.

Reik, Theodor. *Listening with the Third Ear.* New York: Grove Press, 1956.

Riesman, David. *The Lonely Crowd.* New Haven, Conn.: Yale University Press, 1950.

Roberts, David E. *Psychotherapy and a Christian View of Man.* New York: Charles Scribner's Sons, 1950.

Rogers, Carl. *Carl Rogers on Encounter Groups.* New York: Harper & Row, 1970.

———. *Client-Centered Therapy.* Boston: Houghton Mifflin Co., 1951.

Rogers, Carl, and Snyder, William U. *A Casebook of Non-Directive Counseling.* Boston: Houghton Mifflin Co., 1947.

Rothstein, David A. "Presidential Assassination Syndrome." *Archives of General Psychiatry,* September 1964, pp. 245–254.

Rubin, Theodore Isaac. *The Angry Book.* New York: Macmillan, 1969.

Saal, Leon. *The Hostile Mind.* New York: Random House, 1954.

Saint Exupéry, Antoine de. *Wind, Sand and Stars.* New York: Harcourt Brace Jovanovich, Inc., 1968.

Sarwer-Foner, G. J. "Patterns of Marital Relationship." *American Journal of Psychotherapy* 17 (January 1963):31–44.

Satir, Virginia. *Conjoint Family Therapy.* Palo Alto, Calif.: Behavioral Science Books, 1954.

———. *People Making.* Palo Alto, Calif.: Science and Behavior Books, 1972.

Schneidman, Edwin S., and Farberow, Norman L. *Clues to Suicide.* New York: McGraw-Hill, 1960.

Schulberg, Herbert, and Sheldon, Alan. "The Probabilities of Crisis and Strategies for Preventive Intervention." *Archives of General Psychiatry,* May 1968, pp. 553–558.

Sheehy, Gail. *Passages: Predictable Crises of Adult Life.* New York: Bantam Books, 1976.

Sherrill, Lewis Joseph. *The Struggle of the Soul.* New York: Macmillan, 1951.

Shirer, William L. *The Rise and Fall of the Third Reich: A History of Nazi Germany.* New York: Simon and Schuster, 1960.

Skinner, B. F. *Beyond Freedom and Dignity.* New York: Bantam Books, 1971.

Smith, Charles Merrill. *How to Become a Bishop without Being Religious.* Garden City, N. Y.: Doubleday & Co., 1965.

Snell, Rosenwald, and Robey. "The Wifebeater's Wife." *Archives of General Psychiatry* 11 (August 1964):107ff.

Spangler, John D. *Pastoral Care of Young Drug Users and Their Families.* Available from: National Council of Churches. 475 Riverside Drive. Room 576. New York, N. Y. 10027.

Stacey, Chalmers L., and DeMartino, Manfred, eds. *Counseling and Psychotherapy with the Mentally Retarded.* Glencoe: Free Press and Falcon's Wing Press, 1957.

Standal, Stanley W., and Corsini, Raymond J. *Critical Incidents in Psychotherapy.* Englewood Cliffs, N. J.: Prentice-Hall, 1959.

Steiner, Claude M. *Games Alcoholics Play.* New York: Grove Press, 1972.

———. *Scripts People Live.* New York: Grove Press, 1974.

Stewart, Charles W. *The Minister as Marriage Counselor.* New York: Abingdon, 1970.

Stubblefield, Harold W. *The Church's Ministry in Mental Retardation.* Nashville: Broadman Press, 1965.

Stuntz, Edgar C. *Review of Games 1962–1970.* A review of TA literature 1962 through 1970 presented at a workshop on 1-9-71 to the Wabash Valley TA Study Group, West Lafayette, Indiana.

Sullivan, Harry Stack. *Clinical Studies in Psychiatry.* New York: W. W. Norton & Co., 1956.

———. *The Interpersonal Theory of Psychiatry.* New York: W. W. Norton & Co., 1953.

———. *The Psychiatric Interview.* New York: W. W. Norton & Co., 1954.

Sulzburger, Carl Fulton. "Psychoanalytic Treatment of the Paranoid Personality." *American Journal of Psychiatry,* July 1955.

Switzer, David K. *The Minister as Crisis Counselor.* Nashville: Abingdon, 1974.

Tarachow, Sidney. *An Introduction to Psychotherapy.* New York: International Universities Press, 1963.

Teicher, Joseph D. "The Enigma of Predicting Adolescent Suicide Attempts." *Ross*

*Timesaver: Feelings & Their Medical Significance.* Columbus, Ohio: Ross Laboratories, 1972.

Verny, Thomas R. *Inside Groups: A Practical Guide to Encounter Groups and Group Therapy.* New York: McGraw-Hill, 1974.

Walker, James Turner. "Pastor-Parishioner Conversations." A research project submitted to the faculty of Louisville Presbyterian Theological Seminary in partial fulfillment of the requirements for the Doctor of Ministry degree, Louisville, Kentucky, 1975.

*Webster's Seventh New Collegiate Dictionary.* Springfield, Mass.: G. & C. Merriam Co., 1963.

Williams, Daniel Day. *The Minister and the Care of Souls.* New York: Harper & Brothers, 1961.

Winter, Gibson. *Love and Conflict.* Garden City, N. Y.: Doubleday & Co., 1958.

Wolberg, Lewis R. *The Technique of Psychotherapy.* New York: Grune & Stratton, 1954.

Wolff, Sulammith. "Group Discussions with Nurses in a Hospital for Alcoholism." *International Journal of Social Psychiatry* 10 (Autumn 1964):301–302.

Wolpe, Joseph. *The Practice of Behavior Therapy.* New York: Pergamon Press, 1969.

Woollams, Stanley; Brown, Michael; and Huige, Kristyn. *Transactional Analysis in Brief.* Ann Arbor, Mich.: Huron Valley Institute, 1974.

Young, Leontine. *Out of Wedlock.* New York: McGraw-Hill, 1954.

Zimbardo, Philip G. *Shyness.* Reading, Mass.: Addison-Wesley, 1977.